Making
WOW
Jewelry

Making WOW Jewelry

TECHNIQUES AND PROJECTS
FOR MAKING A STATEMENT

GAY ISBER
WITH FASHION PHOTOS BY
CANDICE GHAI

Fox Chapel
PUBLISHING
www.FoxChapelPublishing.com

Dedicated to my kind and patient husband, Kevin McMillan, who never seems to mind that our home is filled with sparkles.
—Gay Isber

All photography by Gay Isber unless noted below.
Photography by Candice Ghai: cover, 2, 8 bottom, 9 right, 31 top, 42 right, 48 bottom, 49 right, 51, 56, 65, 71, 74, 82, 88, 98, 101, 107, 113, 120, 125, 130, 135, 140, 147, 151, 156, 163, and 167
Shutterstock.com images: 19 top right by Tatiana linni; 36 bottom by Picsfive
Flaticon.com images: skill level icon (first occurrence page 50) by Smartline; time icon (first occurrence page 50) by Smashicons; safety notes icon (first occurrence page 50) by Freepik
Pngtree.com images: gold texture pages 9 and 49 by venkatesh venky
Page 135: Dress designed by Sally Daneshjou (sallydaneshjoucollection.com)

ISBN 978-1-4971-0002-2

Library of Congress Control Number:2019003290

To learn more about the other great books from Fox Chapel Publishing, or to find a retailer near you, call toll-free 800-457-9112 or visit us at *www.FoxChapelPublishing.com*.

We are always looking for talented authors. To submit an idea, please send a brief inquiry to acquisitions@foxchapelpublishing.com.

Printed in Singapore
First printing

Ready to WOW?

Whether you are already an experienced jewelry maker or are just familiar with the basics, this book will help you develop the skills you need to make some truly eye-catching pieces. Other crafters will beg to know what techniques you used to create glimmering gem window charms, beetle wing–embedded bracelets, and crystal-encrusted necklaces.

Some projects in this book will teach you how to use new products you may have never heard of to achieve effects you didn't think were possible, and some projects will just use tried-and-true materials and techniques in creative and intriguing ways. You can customize many of these projects to be more or less attention-grabbing, but even a small ring or a single bangle can have the wow factor that this book is all about.

With projects ranging from earrings, necklaces, and rings to crowns, bracelets, and tassels, you'll learn how to colorize crystals, incorporate feathers, create reusable molds, cast with resin, embed in clay, sew with wire, and more. Plus, throughout the jewelry glamor shots in this book, you'll see a lot of extra pieces of jewelry that aren't covered as step-by-step projects. But here's the secret: by the time you learn all the techniques covered and make all the projects, you'll be fully equipped to make these other pieces, too, or simply be inspired by them to make your own custom creations. You'll be able to apply your new skills to create oodles of striking jewelry items and accessories.

So read on to learn how you can make stunning, wearable works of art that will really make people say, "Wow!"

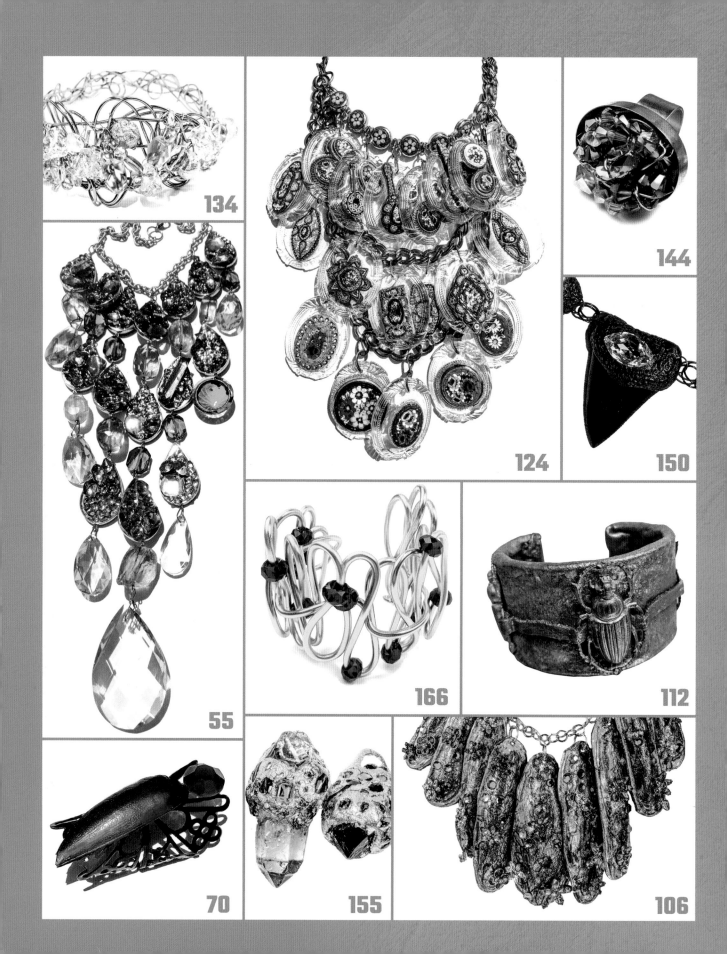

134

124

144

150

55

166

112

70

155

106

Making WOW Jewelry

Contents

PART 1:
GETTING STARTED

Before you start any of the projects in this book, you'll want to review the variety of topics covered in this section. Some sections cover those basic essentials you may need a refresher on, like creating bead links; others focus on specific materials like epoxy clay or techniques like mold making; and still others give you things to think about while creating your designs, like the role color plays. Return to this part of the book as needed for more inspiration and guidance!

"Fashion fades, only style remains the same."
— Coco Chanel

all that glitters

My Story

I have been teaching jewelry design, jewelry making, and entrepreneurial skills at Austin Community College since 2012; I love teaching others how to create beautiful things. It is a passion for me, and this book is a continuation of those classes and that passion. But I didn't start out in jewelry.

I remember the first time I added "artist" to my tax return. I was twenty-eight years old, and it was a eureka moment for me, because I was finally putting a stamp on what I was and had been my entire life. Ever since I was a little girl, I had been a maker of things. By the time I was twenty-eight, I had gone through my glass period, my ceramic period, my collage period, and my copper period, and was smack dab in the middle of my painting period.

Due to a twist in life and a new marriage, I moved from Texas to Waterloo, Ontario,

with my sons. For the first year, I couldn't legally work, but that allowed me the free time to rehab our house, work on paintings, and begin dabbling in jewelry making, despite no training in the craft. At one point, I gave an early bracelet I made to a friend, who showed another friend, and pretty soon I was designing a necklace for a major company! I designed a velvet ribbon with a barrel clasp that had three lobster claws with color-coordinated beads dangling from them. I needed to make 9,000 of these necklaces, so I quickly put an ad in the local newspaper for workers. I bought wire, beads, ribbon, and commercial-sized cookie sheets to keep the beads organized on my dining room table. I called it Project Dingle Dangle. At this point, I still did not know about head pins, eye pins, or how to make an earring. Some of my workers knew more about making jewelry than I did. We all worked hard on those necklaces for three intense weeks and had a lot of fun.

After that, I kept on making jewelry independently, and not much later, I happened upon a sturdy 1920s electrical switching building for sale. It was so dirty, wrecked, and ugly that my friends thought I was crazy to buy it, but I saw the potential. I sold my house and bought the building. I had great ideas for revamping it but a

The fateful design from Project Dingle Dangle!

The interior of the building served as my store and studio and home.

tight budget, so I hired talented but down-on-their-luck men from a local soup kitchen line to help me. In just six months, we created my vision of a happy and creative store/studio/home, a space full of light, beads, happiness, color, and joy.

I called my new home The Sugar Factory and Gay Isber's Design Lab. All the jewelry we sold was handmade by me or my helpers. The first floor was the store and my office, featuring an open floor plan with plenty of room for bracelet-making parties and jewelry displays, and I lived on the top floor. The bracelets we made at the bracelet-making parties here were called Sugar Springs. Guests would make memory wire bracelets using a color-grouped mix of vintage and new beads while sipping their drinks and nibbling on their snacks.

Bracelet-making parties held at my studio/home were always a blast.

The millions of beads were set out on long tables on cookie trays and grouped by color. It was very therapeutic to run your hands through all those beads. I loved those parties.

A few years later, when I outgrew the space, I relocated to a two-story penthouse in downtown Toronto. I adored the floor-to-ceiling windows that flooded the rooms with light, the catwalks, the white marble floors, and the mirrored walls. It was as if Zsa Zsa Gabor and I had designed the space together. It was a perfect place for jewelry making, hosting parties, and living large. I called it The Sugar Factory in the Sky. I will always cherish my time there in the core of a wonderful city.

A few years later, my sons returned to the United States for jobs and the military, so I decided to open a third shop in the creative city of Austin, Texas, closer to my hometown and to my family. I found a large, dilapidated store with an older home attached to the back. I knew I could transform it like I had my first building; I wanted to continue working and living under one roof. I called this third home The Sugar Factory on Koenig. I transformed it with glittering artworks, fanciful chandeliers, and a large white studio that looked onto the street through giant windows.

I recently made the switch to simply working from home with no storefront space, but through all these moves to different homes and studios, there is one thing that has always been true: I love making jewelry, teaching people how to make jewelry, and sharing the beautiful items we've created with the world. So hold onto your hats and let's make some jewelry together!

Sugar ♡

P.S. Are you hungry for more photos and inspiration? Join me on social media; you'll find me as Sugar Gay Isber and Making Wow Jewelry on Facebook, Instagram, and many other sites.

Thinking about Color

Color is a very important and inspiring part of the jewelry-making process.

I love color; I was born with an artist's eyes, and color has always mattered to me. If there were such a thing as perfect color pitch, like with sounds, I would have it. If you are like me, then welcome to the club. But even if you're not, you can learn some basics about color that will serve you well in your jewelry making.

When I first started making jewelry seriously, you could buy great aqua quartz beads. I bought so many that it filled a five-gallon (19-liter) bowl. Now when I try to buy these beautiful beads, though, they are hard to find. **Colors are cyclical.** One day my aqua quartz beads will be available again, but even in my travels to China and India I only spotted a few handfuls. I am hopeful that this color will make a comeback. Remember this when you find beads in a color you adore. Stock

Does this necklace make you hungry?

Blue sells great.

Purple is quite powerful.

Yellow is attention grabbing and often provides high contrast.

up, because you may not be able to find that exact shade or bead again for a while.

Another thing to keep in mind when choosing colors for a design is that **color can powerfully affect our perceptions and moods**. Companies spend plenty of money studying how color motivates us. For example, McDonald's uses red and yellow for specific reasons: red to make us eat quickly and yellow to make us feel happy. Read up on the studied effects of various colors so that you know what your jewelry might be evoking in people. Ask your friends and family to tell you about their favorite colors. Ask them why they like what they like. Colors can tell you a lot about individuals. If you're making a piece for a special someone, consult them about what they like and why.

If you don't know your favorite color—or even if you think you do—look into your closet, visually remove all of the black, and notice what color you see most. The answer might surprise you. I wear a lot of black because it is easy, but I love many colors. Aqua is my absolute favorite color—I get distracted watching movies or TV shows when anything aqua or teal shows up. **Blue** is, in fact, the most liked of all of the colors, and men especially like blue more than any other color. It is the color of our sky and water, so we are surrounded by blues in the natural world. In the jewelry world, blues sell great. I have seen women crawl over things to get their hands on aqua jewelry.

Another popular, powerful color is **purple**. Purple is a combination of blue and red (a power color, meaning stop, pay attention, and the color of blood, which is life). Purple-loving people will buy almost anything in their color. I always try to work a purple piece into a collection, as I know it will be a good seller.

Yellow is a very interesting color. It's not a common color, because it is harder to sell. Think about yellow cars, other than taxis. When was the last time you saw one? Yellow and black are the two most contrasting colors; that is why caution

Metallics, like other colors, often trend cyclically.

When do you think this necklace would sell best?

road signs are in yellow and black, as they are the easiest colors to see together from far away. Yellow is nature's combination color; you might see many colors in your garden, but yellow is almost always present (such as in the centers of flowers). Even one or two yellow beads will make your piece pop.

And then you have **metallics**: mainly gold, copper, and silver, plus fun alternatives like rose gold and bronze. For the longest time, I created almost everything in silver and forgot about copper or gold. Don't do that—use everything you have available to you. Currently, the style pendulum has swung back around, and gold is back in style. Rose gold and copper are becoming ever more popular. People need to have a reason to spend their money on new things, so we are often influenced by what is trending. Some of my clients resist the trends and are stuck in the silver era. That's okay, though—silver will be a trending color again soon enough. It is also a good idea to blend metallics. There really is no rule against adding a gold lobster claw and gold jump rings to a silver chain. It is just part of your design. Embrace trying new things. You might hit upon a truly mesmerizing combination!

I'm not going to exhaustively analyze every color, but hopefully this examination of a few key players has made you think about the role color plays in your jewelry. I'll leave you with one last word of advice: remember that **colors are seasonal**. It is hard to get people to buy red and green combination jewelry unless it's Christmas. Pastels are mostly sold in spring. Neon colors are great for summer. Browns, mustards, burgundies, and forest greens all sell better in the fall. Try tailoring your designs to the season you're in.

Don't be afraid to mix different metals like silver and gold.

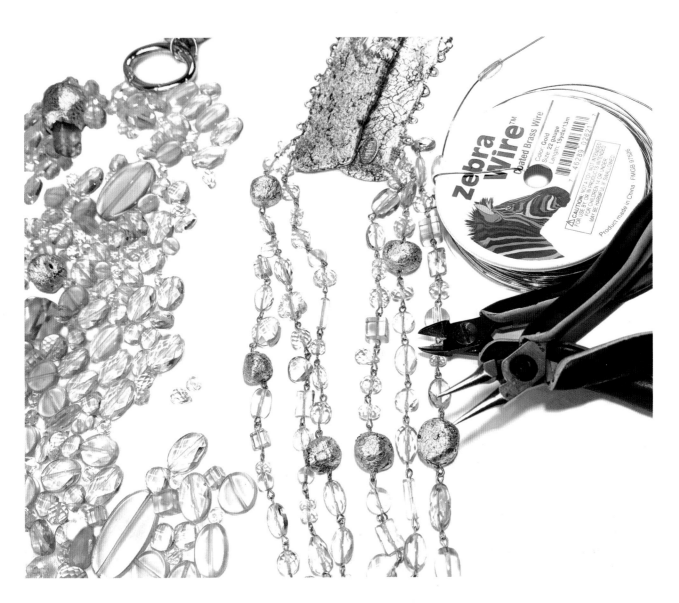

Connecting Beads with Wire

Stringing beads onto a wire or thread is pretty self-explanatory, but also somewhat limiting. It's not that you can't make beautiful things that way; you'll see things strung in this book. But creating **bead links** is more interesting and requires a bit more effort. A bead link is simply a bead (or beads) collected on a short piece of wire, usually with a wire loop rolled on each end. Connecting beads by creating bead links is one of the most basic jewelry-making skills you will learn. This includes bending and looping wire as well as using jump rings. You'll often need to use this skill to connect your clasps to your finished pieces. Once

you have mastered the skill of creating bead links, sometimes called the rosary style of linking, you can make anything. It really is as relaxing as knitting once you get the hang of it. Follow along with the tutorial on page 19 to learn all the basics you'll need.

Keep in mind what you are connecting the bead link to, as this will help you determine the **size of the loop**. If you are connecting a bead link to a chain, then the loop must be big enough to go through a chain link. If you are connecting it to another bead link, then you will probably want all the loops on the bead links to be the same size.

You can always go back and make a loop smaller by slightly opening the link and trimming it, then closing it again. You can also use your pliers to straighten any misshapen links.

The **size of the wire** you'll use to connect beads will depend on the size of the beads. Bigger beads require lower-gauge wire, like an 18-gauge wire, which is strong but harder to bend with your fingers—so I don't recommend starting out with it. If you are making earrings or using smaller beads, then 22-gauge wire could be perfect. (Read more about wire and wire gauge on page 22.)

Buy a good pair of **round-nose pliers** and **flush cutters** (wire cutters); some of the cheaper tools are like working with chopsticks. Although I do treat myself to a fresh pair of cutters about once a year, my pliers are like fingers to me now, and I break out in a sweat if I can't find them for even a minute. If you want to, you can buy a special kind of pliers called rosary chain pliers, which are round-nose pliers with a flush cutter included, making the bead linking process even faster. But you should always have a standard pair of round-nose pliers in your jewelry-making kit. **Straight pliers** (or chain-nose pliers) are also useful depending on how you are assembling your jewelry or what specific wires/beads/findings (i.e., clasps, chains, etc.) you are using. In general for the projects in this book, I use round-nose pliers.

Keep in mind these general beading tips, which apply no matter what you're doing with your beads:

◊ Rest your forearms on the edge of the table. This grounds you so your hands can work freely in the air. Center your body over your arms so you are aligned with your work.

◊ Cover your work surface with a somewhat textured white cloth. You can see the colors more clearly, and it keeps the beads from rolling around like they would on a hard tabletop.

◊ Beads with wide holes and tiny beads are not great for beginners. They are simply trickier to work with; you can master them after you have a few beaded projects under your belt.

◊ Make sure that your beads are clean; wash them with hot water and soap if they have been handled a lot.

In order to follow this tutorial, you'll need a variety of small and large beads, flush cutters, pliers, 20- or 22-gauge wire, a length of chain, jump rings, and a lobster clasp. When it actually comes time to make specific projects with bead links, you may need some or all of these supplies.

HOW TO OPEN JUMP RINGS

Before we get started, it's important that you know the basic rule for opening and closing a jump ring. Shown to the left is the correct method; to the right is the incorrect method. Use a pair of pliers gripped on each side of the jump ring's opening to direct each side away from the other in a vertical orientation. Do not simply pull the opening straight apart, as this will weaken the metal and potentially break it. Think **twist open**, not pull apart.

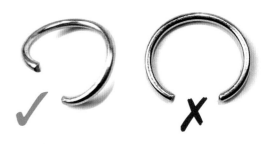

CREATING BEAD LINKS

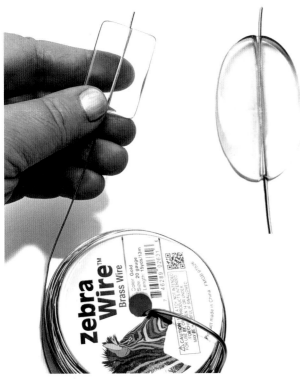

1. Thread a bead onto the wire and hold it in your left hand. You'll need about ½" (1.3cm) of wire to protrude from the top of the bead. Do not cut the other end of the wire off of the spool yet.

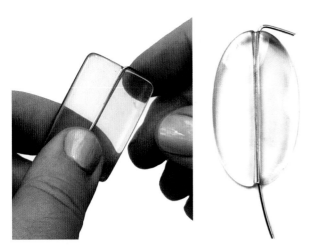

2. Bend the short end of the wire 90 degrees, into a right angle. You can push it over with your fingertip, or use pliers if doing it manually hurts your hands.

3. If your wrist could rotate 360 degrees, you could do this in one step, but our wrists don't work that way. Therefore, completing the loop is typically a two-step movement. Use your pliers to create a J shape at the tip of the bent wire, using a rolling motion.

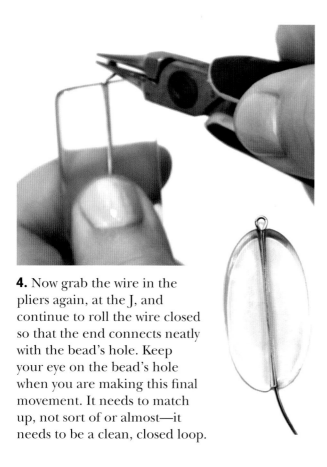

4. Now grab the wire in the pliers again, at the J, and continue to roll the wire closed so that the end connects neatly with the bead's hole. Keep your eye on the bead's hole when you are making this final movement. It needs to match up, not sort of or almost—it needs to be a clean, closed loop.

6. Once the first bead link is finished, start on the next. Before you close the second loop of the second bead link, link it into one of the other bead link's loops. Only then should you close the second loop of the second bead link. You've connected your first two bead links!

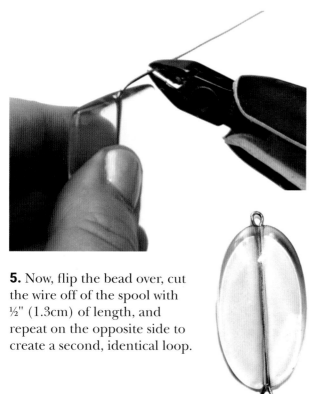

5. Now, flip the bead over, cut the wire off of the spool with ½" (1.3cm) of length, and repeat on the opposite side to create a second, identical loop.

7. As you can see here, both loops should be completely closed and not overlapping. The loops should be approximately the same size. You can use your pliers to adjust the loops if necessary.

8. Continue linking beads this way until you are happy with your result. Check all of the links once you are completely finished by holding the piece up to eye level and allowing it to dangle. If you see anything too big or crooked, you can correct it.

9. The easiest way to connect the ends of your bead link chain to a finishing chain is by using jump rings; it creates a nice, clean finish. Sometimes, you can connect the bead links directly to the chain using the loops the same way each bead link is connected to the next. Remember to open the jump rings properly (see page 18).

10. If you're making something with a clasp, cut the chain and attach the clasp (such as this lobster clasp) to one end. Make sure the clasp is the right size to close through the chain. If the clasp is too chunky for the gaps in the chain, the closure won't work.

Whipping Up with Wire

Wire will be the basis for a lot of your jewelry. One of the most important decisions you'll need to make when creating with wire is what gauge to use. **Wire gauge** is measured from thickest (lower numbers) to thinnest (higher numbers). Use the thickest wire (the lowest gauge) that your beads can accommodate. Most natural gems and freshwater pearls require much finer wire and are better for stringing projects, since fine wire is often quite delicate. 20-gauge wire is a good choice for necklaces, and sometime 18-gauge wire if the design will work or if you need it to be really strong. Men's and children's jewelry are good projects in which to use 18-gauge wire. 22-gauge wire is a good choice for smaller, daintier projects and earrings.

You can also make stiff items like bracelets out of thicker wire, like 12-gauge and even 6-gauge wire. You can use thin, threadlike wire to "sew" beads and embellishments onto thicker-gauge bases. I particularly like Oasis brand floral arranging wire for thick wire, because it is soft on the fingers but strong. It also comes in great colors. You don't have to stick with silver and gold wire; you can buy **wire in every color** imaginable. There are great colors in Zebra Wire™ brand wire,

which is coated copper and is stiffer. It doesn't bend as easily, but you can work with it. For general use, look for aluminum wire.

When working with a spool of wire, there's nothing more frustrating than the wire **unspooling** into a big mess. To keep the spool of wire from uncoiling, wrap a piece of random wire through the center hole and knot it closed with your fingers before you start using it. Containing the wire like this will save you time and stress.

Many projects in this book utilize wire as a key and focal part of the design; see pages 134, 139, 146, and 166.

My spool trick: create a wire wrap to keep your wire from unspooling.

Bracelets can also be made simply of wire with beads.

♡SUGAR STORY

I used to carry a spool of aluminum fencing wire and a pair of pliers to entertain myself on trips. I made all sorts of trinkets with this plain, boring old wire. It was my signature fidget cure. But I didn't start adding beads to my wire works until much later, somewhat by accident! When I was living in Ontario, my large paintings were being featured in art shows, but I also wanted to sell an easier-to-buy product that had the exuberance of my paintings, so I decided to design a tassel. After trial and error and some problems sourcing pieces I needed, I ended up with a whole bunch of small glass circles that I couldn't use for my tassel idea. But then, sitting in front of the TV one night, I decided to string those circles onto some wire, and I whipped up a bracelet! I quickly hopped onto eBay to buy vintage beads, and with those beads I created a few dozen bracelets that I dubbed Traffic Stoppers. They were a smash hit at my next art show. These were some of the earliest pieces of jewelry I ever made.

You can make interesting bracelets out of nothing but a bunch of wire.

This is the first bracelet that I created, so long ago.

Customizing Cuff Bracelets

Bracelets were the first kind of jewelry I ever created. They started my career, so I am always happy to make more. But my bracelets have evolved greatly over time. The first bracelet I created was made from beads and wire (see page 23). It was designed to shake and rattle as an attention-getter. I called it the Traffic Stopper.

After making other bracelets like this, I tried making cuff-style bracelets. I created the frames with wire, which was effective but not easy or consistent. The wire was not really strong enough to keep its shape. What I needed was a ready-made frame!

One of my early hand-formed cuff bracelets.

Later, I created a bracelet using all Swarovski crystals. My beads were getting ever better, but the result was still lacking a polished feel.

Finally, after years of making my own freestyle bracelets this way, I found a ready supply of pre-made cuff bracelet frames in gold and silver tones and in a few sizes and styles.

By using pre-made cuffs as your base, you can make your own beautiful cuff bracelets with anything you can imagine. You can use all kinds of chains, resin, beads, and just plain wire to decorate these cuffs. Read on for a gallery showcasing some diverse ideas for making cuff bracelets. For a step-by-step cuff bracelet project, see page 87.

An early Swarovski bracelet.

The wonderful frame that would change my bracelet-making game.

I used this basic pre-made frame to create something wonderful. I painted the frame with layers of red nail polish and used red wire to "sew" on Swarovski crystals in various red shades for an all-red look. Talk about your wow effect! This is an easy bracelet for all levels, as it is much like sewing.

A painted frame matches the beads for an all-over wow color effect.

Cuff Bracelet Gallery

Curve some metal filigree pieces with your fingers and pliers and then "sew" them onto a frame with 24-gauge wire. Add a few pearls to glam it up.

Here, only the middle part of the bracelet frame gets colorful pearls and a few sparkly beads.

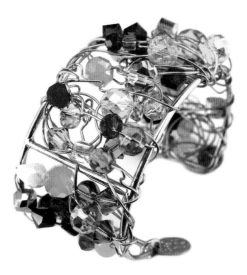

This cuff uses a few dozen beads and 20-gauge brass wire, so it is strong enough to hold its shape. Just think "random"; with your pliers, grab the wire in places to give it a little half twist, which will both tighten it and add squiggles to the design. Super easy!

These beads are made from Roman-era glass. The wrapping is done with 24-gauge wire, and a few sparkles on one edge make it art.

The translucent green glass beads of this bracelet make art when the morning sun passes through them. It's art making art . . . with a little help from our sun!

Look for creative ways to change the ingredients of your bracelets. Here I used split rings instead of a lot of beads. I threw in a few sparkly, colorful beads to give it a little variety and pizzazz.

This cuff is made with small, gold-toned beads and a few small sparklies thrown in. All the beads are about 4mm in size.

These glass tubes are perfect for making an extra-large bracelet.

This silver pearl and black diamond assortment on a silver frame truly shines.

Chunky gold wire makes a standalone statement on a gold frame.

Red coral makes for a high-drama cuff bracelet.

Natural semiprecious stones and perhaps a few sparkles are perfect for cuff bracelets. These are (from top to bottom) lapis, rose quartz, and amazonite beads.

An assortment of Swarovski crystals in various colors covering the cuff frame make these bracelets sparkle like crazy! Try them in fuchsia and bright yellow. They knock your socks off with sparkle.

Adding Sparkle

I remember the first time that I put a few Swarovski crystals on a bracelet. I had been resisting using them because I thought that my beads were beautiful enough. And then I added a sprinkle of Swarovskis, and that first bracelet instantly sold. It really is all about the sparkle, baby.

Sparkle matters. It's eye-catching, mesmerizing, and tantalizing. It adds glitz and glamour. And it's not necessarily an artificial effect; think of all the sparkling stones in nature, or even the way light reacts with water. You can make both high-fashion and natural effects with sparkle. I highly recommend you try to work some sparkle into your pieces. You want that wow factor, don't you?

If you're searching for extra sparkle, keep an eye out for the designation **AB**. This stands for Aurora Borealis, and it means there is a rainbow coating on the crystals that adds an extra colorful flash. Any kind of bead or crystal can be AB. AB2X is a code for two times the AB, meaning the

coating is all the way around the bead, not on just part of it. AB isn't the only coating out there, but it's the most common. If you are doing a project that requires crystals, order a mix of non-AB, AB, and AB2X. It makes for more interesting pieces.

On eBay (or at thrift shops), you can also purchase **vintage crystal necklaces**, and sometimes the crystals are in near-perfect condition. Boy, do these sparkle. Wash any vintage crystal beads with hot, soapy water and then towel dry them. After all these years, they will be dirty, even if your eye can't see it. The difference between the before and after is amazing. (Note: Don't wash vintage pearls, as it could loosen the coating.)

You can also buy a great many vintage Swarovski flat backs from online dealers, usually the type that have a **metallic coating** on their backside so they sparkle when they are embedded in clay or resin. If a crystal is without a backing, you do get a sparkle on the top, but it will take on the color of whatever is beneath it. If you have great flat backs

Preciosa crystals, like these drops, are a great not-too-expensive but not-too-cheap crystal choice.

that don't have the metallic coating on the back, use a gold metallic paint marker and coat them yourself. It might not be perfect, but it does help. You can also use gold nail polish to create this effect.

There are many tiers of **crystal quality** out there, from cheap to expensive. My favorite brand of crystal producers is Swarovski (made in Austria), which offers premium products. They come in inventive colors, coatings, and shapes. If you're selling your jewelry, the Swarovski name will help you sell. They are not the only company that makes sparkle, though. If you are just starting out, try any of a variety of brands of Chinese crystals, which are cheap and cheery. When you're ready to take it up a notch, try something like Preciosa crystals (made in the Czech Republic). I have made some amazing pieces with Preciosa crystals, especially their crystal drops. They come in many beautiful colors and sizes. Finally, you can graduate to Swarovski.

Sparkle adds light and movement. But **actual movement** is a step up from just plain sparkle. I remember the first time I saw a Fabergé collection at a museum. It's true, the diamonds and gems added a ton of eye-popping sparkle, but one of the crowns had a part of it on little springs called a trembler. The crown was created so that the movement of its trembling bits would catch everyone's attention, even from across the room. Real movement trumps sparkle. So try adding movement to some of your pieces: little rings on wire that can move (I call these "fidgeters"), circles that slide over smaller beads, beads with openings that allow you to insert a bead inside of them—all of these result in a non-static creation. Make your sparklies move, and you'll compound the effect!

Using Epoxy Clay

When I first started working with clay, I used your standard polymer bakeable clay, the kind you probably used as a kid. But after a lot of not-so-ideal results (see page 32), I finally discovered a product that is much better suited to jewelry: epoxy clay. Epoxy clay opened up my clay jewelry creativity and took it to the next level. I am in love with this product, and you will be, too, once you try it.

Epoxy clay is a **self-hardening clay** that you make by mixing two parts (A and B). You usually have about two to three hours of workable time with the clay before it begins to harden. Once it hardens, it is extremely durable, almost as hard as stone, and strong enough to hold almost anything in place. It has no odor after hardening. Metallic leaf adheres to it perfectly. You can easily seal it, but you don't have to. You can rub it to a soft sheen, model it, mold it, and stick things into it. If I were a member of any fan club, it would be for epoxy clay.

There are many projects in this book that utilize epoxy clay, so read this section carefully! The projects can be found on pages 61, 64, 73, 78, 81, 97, 100, 119, 129, 150, 155, and 171.

Several companies make epoxy clays, and you can buy small packages for your first try with the product. Swarovski makes an epoxy clay called Ceralun; another company makes Crystal Clay™; and there are many more. One of my favorite products is Apoxie® Sculpt from a company called Aves Studio.

The clay typically comes in a few **standard colors**, not the huge rainbow that bakeable clay is available in, but you can blend the clays together to make almost any color. There is a magical shade in the Aves Studio palette called Super White, which you can mix with other, darker colors to create lovely, soft pastels. For master color mixing, download the color-mixing chart on the Aves Studio website (*www.avesstudio.com/12_color_chart_pantone.pdf*), which is linked to Pantone colors. You can even mix in some mica powders or glitters to add a little frosting.

This quality crown would never have been possible with regular oven-baked clay.

You can embed virtually anything in epoxy clay.

♥ SUGAR STORY

One year a company hired me to create a collection of jewelry. I spent a month making more than 300 small models (to be manufactured later) out of all different colors of clay. At the end, I thought that I would turn the mishmash of hard work into something cohesive, so I spray-painted a big group of the charms with gold paint. But I had forgotten, in my haste, to seal the charms first, so the paint would not firm up. What a mess! It was a hard lesson to learn.

I really loved working with clay, though, so I didn't stop there. Next I created a lovely crown and jewelry set using bakeable clay, pressing in Swarovski jewels before baking it. Unfortunately, the clay was not strong enough to hold the stones—the pieces came back from the photographer with a whole bag of sparkle that had fallen out. I loved clay, but bakeable clay had its limits, and I knew I couldn't keep using it for my work. Then, by chance, I stumbled upon epoxy clay. Sometimes you just have to keep looking and wait for others to invent the product that you need!

My ill-fated gold charms made from bakeable clay.

ESSENTIALS FOR WORKING WITH EPOXY CLAY

◊ Wear gloves to mix it, as it is a chemical, and it is very sticky in the mixing process.

◊ Make sure your space is well ventilated.

◊ Work on a surface that is covered with disposable plastic, or, if you make sure to clean up quickly, you can work on a non-disposable plastic surface.

◊ For the best precision, weigh the A and B parts separately, on a mailing or kitchen digital scale—eyeballing isn't an exact science. I messed up once by not paying attention and mixed two A parts together instead of A and B parts. This makes nothing but a messy mistake that you only figure out when it doesn't harden.

◊ If you don't mix the two parts thoroughly enough to ensure that they are totally incorporated, you could have areas within your piece that never harden. So mix and then mix some more. Follow the directions to blend the clay until all the gray is gone and there are no streaks. Don't rush the mixing process and you won't be disappointed.

◊ If you don't use all of your mixed clay, it will eventually harden, so don't waste it: roll it into a ball, poke a hole through it with a piece of wire, and make a bead.

◊ Keep plenty of baby wipes on hand to clean up as you go. You can wipe stones and other items embedded in the clay with a baby wipe to clean off fingerprints and stray clay, but do not wipe the clay; small white fibers will stick to the clay and ruin the perfect finish.

◊ Wash your hands thoroughly after each use. Clean up your work area and tools immediately—otherwise you will have hard-as-rock bits to pry off later.

Playing with Bugs

I have always been a bug girl; I loved learning how to collect bugs and study them. I will never forget the first time I used a little microscope to see the scales on a butterfly's wings. I was hooked.

Bug and animal jewelry goes back to the earliest times. Think about scarab beetles, for example; their history in jewelry is many thousands of years old. Creating jewelry with the image of a bug, the shape of a bug, or real bugs is simply part of our global history of art. Look for ancient jewelry references and then look at images that famous brands, like Cartier, have created to inspire your own jewelry making.

There are many ways to **source bugs** for your jewelry. You can purchase bugs through collectors and also collect your own in your backyard, using a white sheet and a strong light at night. You can kill the bugs humanely by freezing them or applying a cotton ball soaked with nail polish remover. Use different containers for each type of bug—don't jumble beetles together with moths, for example. Only collect what you need—you can always collect more. Make sure you are not collecting any endangered species, either—there are many protected butterflies in North America, for example. Put a paper towel in each container with the bugs to absorb any moisture, and make sure they are thoroughly dried out for several weeks before use. Their little legs, antennae, and wings are fragile, so handle with care.

Internet marketplaces such as eBay are wonderful for sourcing bugs, but they can be very expensive. The shipping costs are usually high, as true collectors will make sure that all export paperwork is in place and that their packaging will withstand traveling through the mail, which you definitely want as a paying customer. Make sure whomever you purchase from is sourcing their bugs responsibly.

If you're squeamish, **plastic bugs** are fun, too! Shop at dollar stores or in toy stores to find what you need. You can use them straight out of the bag.

The original butterfly crown.

♥ SUGAR STORY

The first time I used bugs in my jewelry was when I was living in Ontario. A new butterfly center was opening nearby, and I wanted to make a collection as a nod to it, so I decided to create a crown made with real butterflies. An Internet search led me to the top bug purveyor in North America, who taught me to use clear nail polish to stiffen the butterflies' wings. I carefully applied antique sequins and glitter to the butterflies and created tiny springs with wire to attach each one to the crown. The effect was magical, as the butterflies seemed to hover and flutter as you moved.

Clear nail polish is your best friend when it comes to using bugs. This product will add a protective layer to the bug's body to help it stay durable. It's especially essential that you cover butterfly wings with a layer of clear polish to preserve their beautiful scales. I like Sally Hanson Hard as Nails clear topcoat.

When it comes to **embellishing** your bugs, you'll want to use glue, paint, and glitter. Wet paint will usually hold the small amounts of glitter that you will use. If the paint is already dry, add a little clear-drying glue to make the glitter stick. Experiment and play. Your bug jewelry will be a conversation starter, and you will soon have a collection of traffic-stopping pieces. Plus, at Halloween, they are must-haves to wear to the office.

Make this buggy project (and several more) starting on page 64.

If bug bodies aren't your thing, you can still take advantage of some of what makes them beautiful by using **insect-inspired paints**. Golden Artist Colors brand makes a line of paints called Interference that were designed by studying butterfly wings to create that beautiful, natural shimmering effect. These paints are amazing and very thick, so a little goes a long way. Look in the paint aisle of your craft store for this and other paints that have an iridescent two-color shine. Many types of nail polish now have that two-tone look, too. Don't be afraid to spend a little more money than you normally would on a nail polish that is really iridescent, because you will use it sparingly, and none is wasted, since the brush never has to be cleaned off. (Nail polish is truly a great tool; see page 35 for more info.)

Here are some fun photos showing a few of the buggy pieces that I have created over the years.

MAKING WOW JEWELRY

My nail polish collection for jewelry making.

Tricks with Nail Polish

Nail polish isn't a traditional artist's or jewelry maker's tool. But I want to highlight it here because I want to give you permission to use any tool without guilt. Nail polish is a perfect example of a "weird" tool that you should totally take advantage of.

There are a few great **benefits** to nail polish:

◊ It comes in many amazing colors, with or without glitter, in glow-in-the-dark versions, in UV-cured styles, and in amazing iridescent and holographic shades.

◊ You can buy it almost anywhere.

◊ It is sold at many price points.

◊ You may already have some in your house. (I am old enough to remember when you always had clear polish in your purse to stop a run in your hose!)

◊ The little brush is perfect for use with jewelry.

◊ It requires no cleanup, unlike regular paints.

35

There are a bunch of **tricks** you can do with nail polish that should immediately convince you to keep it on hand. For example, if you are creating something with a black wire, and the coating gets nicked in the process of making the piece, a quick touch of black nail polish makes the nick disappear like magic. Another example: some porcelain beads have white cores that aren't too pleasing on a finished piece. So, before you use them, color in the centers with a drop of polish that matches the bead to make them look more finished.

You can also quickly **alter the color** of any bead or jewelry finding with nail polish to suit your needs. If you're trying to match a color, take the item to the store when you shop for the nail polish. You will see many examples in this book of me doctoring up items with a bit of paint. Don't be afraid to use polish to create whatever effect you want. One time I coated an entire necklace of Swarovski pearls with a slightly sparkly gloss polish because the pearls' original coating was too matte and it just didn't look right with the project I was making. It took no time, dried quickly, and I loved the result. Don't lie to people about your use of nail polish; in fact, you should point out that you took the time to create your unique vision of loveliness. We're artists; we create.

To add to the drama of this black-beaded piece, I painted the silver frame jet black with nail polish before adding the beads.

The one thing that I have never seen on the market, anywhere, is the paint that is used to coat manmade pearls. Thinking of all the things that would be great if **pearlized** makes my head swoon! Pearly nail polishes can be a close substitute for this. Take a bad bead you were going to throw away, add a few coats of a topcoat, then a pearly white, then another coat of gloss, and that bead is now a stunner.

I **store** my polishes on my workbench on a pretty, high-edged silver tray. The edge keeps them from toppling when they are carried to another location. It has definitely saved me a few times. A cardboard box would work, too. The point is to keep your polishes close and use them as needed. So next time you see a sale on polish in the cosmetics aisle, find some great colors that you love. Your nails might like it, but so will your jewelry!

You can make molds out of so many different things.

Making Molds

When I discovered mold making, using just a simple kit of a two-part silicone, it was like I discovered lightning in a bottle. It blasted open doors that I never dreamed I could open. You can take any object and make a mold of it to replicate it over and over. It's addicting and perfect for so many projects.

To make a mold, you use a **silicone mold-making putty product**, which typically consists of A and B substances that you mix together and then press an item into. To make copies of the

♡TIP

You can use molds made from Castin'Craft® putty for food and ice, but only if you haven't made nonedible items in the mold already. If you want a mold for the kitchen, make it and keep it exclusively for use in the kitchen. And always read and follow the manufacturer's instructions before using any mold with food.

item in the resulting mold, you use resin or clay (sometimes requiring mixing—see page 31). I like making purple molds out of EasyMold® Silicone Putty because it gives a shiny surface to the copied item. Another product, Amazing Mold Putty by Alumilite, creates a yellow mold and leaves a matte finish when you use resin in it. Choose whichever effect you prefer.

Molds have **tons of applications**. They are great for recreating heirlooms; you could make a copy of Grandma's favorite charm so that every family member has one, for example. Molds are also great for colorizing fossils into crazy colors. Start making a mental list—or a physical pile—of things that might be fun to make a mold of. Once you have made your mold, you can use resins and clays in the mold along with mica powders, foils, and films to make the results even more fun.

Before making a mold, be aware of **copyright laws**. Anything that you buy new today might be copyrighted, meaning you can't necessarily take any object, make a mold of it, and then create copies to sell. If you carve an object yourself from bakeable clay, epoxy clay, or anything else, though, it's unequivocally yours! Try buying ancient fossils or antique/vintage items, or make your own items, so copyrights are less of an issue.

I learned how to make molds by making mistakes, trying hard, pushing the limits, experimenting, and enjoying the process. You will, too! Once you make your first mold and then create something with it, you will be hooked.

On page 50 you will find a project that takes you step by step through the creation of a mold. Also read through the lists of tips on page 39.

If possible, store your molds with the mold-making item in them, to help preserve the mold shape over time.

See page 50 for a step-by-step project that begins by showing you how to create a mold.

ESSENTIALS FOR MAKING MOLDS

◊ Always carefully read and follow the manufacturer's instructions.

◊ Have everything out and ready, as you only have a minute or so once you start blending the two parts together before the mold material will start to set. Be organized so you don't waste any product.

◊ Wear gloves! Making silicone molds involves chemicals and a chemical reaction.

◊ Always wash your hands after working with the product.

◊ Work in a well-ventilated area.

◊ Work on a plastic or silicone surface. You can work on top of a plastic bag that has a piece of cardboard or cardstock in it so that you can easily move the mold and to prevent it from sticking to paper.

◊ For your first mold, start with something small; that way, if you do mess up, you haven't wasted much of the kit.

◊ When making the mold impression, don't press the object in so deep that it goes down all the way through to the plastic bag and creates a hole. If you accidentally do this early enough in the process, you might be able to quickly roll the material back into a ball and try again.

◊ Try to keep the object flat when you press it in, so it isn't a lopsided mold. Remind yourself to push straight down.

◊ Be aware of the thickness of your mold. A mold only needs to be about ¼" (0.5cm) thicker than the object you are molding. More than that is a waste of product.

◊ If you can store the object in its mold, the mold will stay in better shape. I store my molds and the original objects in clear, plastic, pint-sized ice cream containers with screw-on tops. You can keep them in zip-top bags, too. Whatever you do, try to keep the molds clean and dust-free.

ESSENTIALS FOR USING MOLDS

◊ The first six items from the list of Essentials for Making Molds apply to using molds, especially when using casting resins and epoxy clays. (Bakeable clay usually doesn't require as much caution and care.)

◊ See page 31 for detailed information on using epoxy clays.

◊ You need to follow many of the same guidelines as epoxy clays when using casting resin.

◊ Wash molds with a drop of soap and water.

Crafting Crowns

I never had a crown as a child, so I don't know where my obsession with crowns came from. I do know that whenever women (and men and children, too!) put on a crown that fits perfectly, it instantly makes them happy. They don't even have to see themselves—they just know there's a fun object on their head, and they seem to love it. I have made crowns, tiaras, and headpieces for dogs, babies, brides, celebrities, royalty, my sons, and friends, and some I made just because I had a vision that had to be created. When normal jewelry might not be the right thing, a crown might do the trick.

On pages 78, 81, 100, 134, and 146, you can learn to make crowns that are real stunners.

Crowns are showstoppers by their very nature; they aren't a kind of jewelry one typically wears!

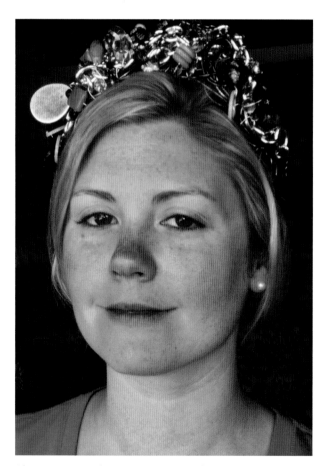

Always try to make a crown suit and fit its wearer's head.

♡ SUGAR STORY

I shipped a crown that I created for my son in the U.S. Navy to him on his first big tour of the Pacific. I had a trinket from my grandfather from WWI that I added to it, along with some anchors and Navy-related stuff (the crown is pictured at left). Months later, he sent back photos and stories of his shipmates and ship's captain all wearing the crown!

A sparkly crown will make you feel like royalty.

TIPS FOR MAKING CROWNS

◊ Crowns and tiaras are not worn like a baseball cap down on your forehead. They are placed on the crown of your head, a little angled and tilted back so you can see the design on the front.

◊ Measure the head for the crown, if possible.

◊ If you can make a crown adjustable, that is even better—and it's possible with wire!

◊ Make sure that nothing will poke or catch on hair—that will totally take the fun out of wearing it.

◊ Gather inspirational photos of crown shapes. When I first started making crowns, I had a book of the Queen of England's jewelry as a reference for shapes.

◊ Try not to make your crowns heavy; nothing is worse than wearing something that hurts.

◊ For bridal headpieces, remember to use pearls; sparkle won't be captured in photos.

◊ Photographing crowns can be a bit tricky. See if you can get a Styrofoam wig head. Since you can only see part of the crown at a time in a single photo, take photos from multiple angles.

♡ SUGAR STORY

I got a funny call one Friday: seven dogs were running for mayor of a small town in northern California, the press was coming the following week for a group photo, and would I make tiaras for each of them and get them there by Tuesday? Of course I would! That Monday, I grabbed a box from under the kitchen table, threw in the crowns, raced to the post office, pushed the box at the shipping clerk, and said, "Please just get these to California by tomorrow!" Later that week, the lady who had given me the job called and said, "They were a hit! And only you would think to put cookies in the box." This stumped me until I realized that the cookies must have already been in the box when I hurriedly tossed the tiaras into it.

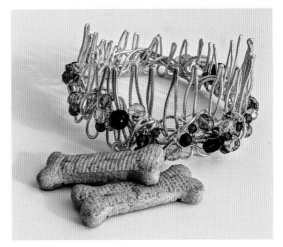

Crowns aren't just for people—they can be for pooches, too!

The Magic of Pearls

Natural pearls begin as a tiny piece of grit inside a mollusk; over time, a natural coating grows around the irritant, and a pearl is formed. I've always had a special affinity for these beauties; I'm a June baby, so pearls are one of my birthstones. I still have my first necklace that had a tiny real pearl in it. My stash of pearls today is very large, as I have been collecting them for almost 20 years.

In ancient times, pearls were more valuable than diamonds or other gems. It was hard work for divers to hold their breath while diving deep into the Mediterranean Sea to find the mollusks that held pearls. Cleopatra famously dissolved a giant pearl in vinegar and drank it just to show her immense wealth. A string of pearls was truly something to be admired.

Fast-forward to today's world. Real pearls are farmed like lettuce. They are still valuable, though, because a lot of work and love go into producing them. Pearls have been **commercialized** into many shapes, and the colors are enhanced with dyes. Nowadays, prices are more reasonable, making pearls accessible to many jewelry makers. I recently purchased a strand of giant white baroque pearls online for $30.

You can also purchase **faux pearls** that are made of acrylic, glass, cotton, or crystal. Corporations like Swarovski have also created amazing pearl coatings that they use on their crystals, making a premium product with a nice weight, a variety of shapes and colors, and great gloss.

Pearls photograph the best—something brides need to realize! Think about it: it is hard to capture sparkle in a photo. The lighting has to be just right. Pearls, on the other hand, can be seen in all their glory with all kinds of lighting conditions and wardrobe colors.

When it comes to creating **strings of pearls**, you can knot them or use wire bead links. (Stringing them straight together is not a good idea, as the pearls will rub against each other and become damaged.) Knotting pearls is not that hard; it just

No doubt about it—I'm a pearl hoarder!

Vintage pearls, like the ones used here, are amazing and unique finds.

requires patience and practice. Once you get good at it, it is like knitting. Nothing moves on your neck quite like a string of knotted pearls. To knot pearls, slide pearls onto thread or thin cord, and simply tie a knot with the thread snug up against each pearl on the strand as you go, creating a small but effective space between each pearl. Wire-linking pearls is a good alternative to knotting (see page 17 for details on this method).

Pearls come in many shapes and sizes.

These are rare cotton pearls from 1950s Japan.

There are several things to remember when deciding on pearls for a project:

◊ Small freshwater pearls have equally small holes. This makes them perfect for stringing on thin threads, but not great for getting wire through.

◊ In the description of a faux pearl, it should say if it is glass or acrylic based (or other). Ambiguity is not a sign of quality.

◊ Acrylic pearls can be great for projects where weight is an issue. A big strand of glass or crystal pearls can be heavy. So if your project is weight sensitive, acrylic is a super solution.

A few projects in this book incorporate pearls; see pages 61 and 119.

Don't be afraid to creatively incorporate pearls with other beads and findings.

Shooting art can be challenging.

Shoot in bright light—natural sunlight if possible.

Photography Tips and Tricks

Whether you want to sell your jewelry or just show off your creations on Instagram, you'll want to take quality photos of your work. A long time ago, I was hiring photographers to take photos of my large artworks. It was expensive. I had to make sure that I owned the rights to those photos. Today I have more than 200,000 photos of my creations, a whole lifetime of photos, backed up in the cloud, on extra storage devices, on a server, and on my computers. If you have the means and motivation, you can get a friend or a professional to photograph your work, but most readers, I know, will be taking their own photos.

Take photos of each piece that you create. Rename the file so it has your name in it and any details to make it easily searchable, instead of using the string of numbers from your camera. For example, one of my filenames is "Gay Isber Shark's Teeth Necklaces Spring 2019." You should include your name in the filename, because you never know where the photos will end up. You can add the name of the item, the collection's name, or the month that you made it to help in future searches.

A **smartphone** can take great photos that you can instantly access to edit on your computer or phone and easily share. If you are shopping for a new phone, get one with a great camera. I also own a great actual camera, but I find I use it less and less. It's up to you what kind of technology works for you. Download your best images to your computer to run them through a photo-editing software such as Picasa or Photoshop.

Take photos **in full sun** for maximum sparkle and color clarity. I recommend that you acquire the same props I use: a white poster board, a white extra-long jewelry display neck, a few white props, and a piece of white foam core that you can quickly grab when it's time for picture-taking. Even in full sun and using a great camera, many photos will have to be edited to some degree to truly showcase the jewelry. If you have the space, create a permanent setup to take photos indoors, which is super handy.

Give your photos good file names to make it easy to find what you need. You don't want to scroll through pages of necklaces to find this particular photo, for example!

WHAT BACKGROUNDS ARE BEST

A word about using black in your jewelry displays and photos: DON'T.

Think of the world-class jewelers: Tiffany & Co, Cartier, Harry Winston, Van Cleef & Arpels, etc. They all use white as the background for displaying their jewelry—and for a good reason. It shows off the color better. There is also a perception bias whereby black displays, boxing, and backgrounds make jewelry pieces seem cheaper and of lesser quality. Also, light gives off sparkle, and a black background sucks up light. You want your jewelry to sparkle, right? So if you are using black neck displays, change them to white or ivory and see your sales increase—period. Amazon wants pure white photo backgrounds for a reason. Take note, and remove all black from your jewelry sales areas.

I was recently invited to critique a jewelry display at an art gallery. They were really proud of the green felt at the bottom of the display. Guess what color the jewelry was—green. You couldn't see the nuanced shades of green in the jewelry; it was totally washed out by the green background. White would have made those greens pop.

White is how you win at photography.

Sourcing Materials

There are a lot of jewelry supply companies and sources out there, from your local craft store to small online retailers to big online retailers. Jewelry makers will have different needs and preferences, but I can definitely make some recommendations for my favorite brands and sources for various kinds of jewelry-making materials. Keep in mind that this isn't an exhaustive list of sources; these are just some of my favorites that you might want to check out.

Local Craft Stores

Enjoy the hunt for amazing beads, gems, and supplies right in your own town! Check out any of your local craft stores. Visit their websites to find a location near you. Some supplies are just more fun to buy when you can see them in person, like paint, casting products, beads, and Beadalon products (another favorite brand of mine). You can pick up basic findings like jump rings whenever you're at your local store. Also keep an eye out for coupons.

Fire Mountain Gems

www.firemountaingems.com

I have had a long relationship with Fire Mountain Gems; I've even met the owners at a conference, and they are just lovely. This is a family-owned business and often holds some amazing sales; you can find interesting items that sometimes cost pennies apiece. I usually load up on Swarovski crystals when they are on sale. Try entering one of the contests. This is a good source for gold, copper, and silver foil.

Amazon

www.amazon.com

There are many resin and molding products available through Amazon. You can find a lot of other findings, beads, and tools here, too.

eBay

www.ebay.com

A well-known Internet retailer, eBay is where you can find treasure (as well as trash). I've used eBay a lot over the years—in fact, I've made over 5,000 purchases. Search for reputable sellers. You will be able to find a lot of great vintage items here.

Aves Studio

www.avesstudio.com

Aves Studio sells handmade epoxy clays that I use throughout this book. It is a family-owned company; the father invented the products and the daughter, Erin, keeps improving them. You can purchase their products in small quantities on various online sources or directly from the company.

There is a large variety of Swarovski pearls and beads available from Fire Mountain Gems. These earrings are made using a variety of sizes of pearls, beads, and components. They are even prettier in person, as they glow and sparkle.

I do love eBay for connecting me to vintage, New Old Stock (NOS) sources. I have long-standing relationships with a few dealers because I keep buying over and over from them. I send them photos of what I made, and they dig up hard-to-find, interesting items for me. A great buy on eBay is vintage chain by the spool. I must have miles of chain by now.

Whenever you find a fossil or small item you might like to use again, make a mold for your collection. Try mixing in dyes for unusual colors or adding mica powders for shimmer and interest.

Nunn Design
www.nunndesign.com
I love using products made in the USA. Nunn Design is a small yet wonderful, woman-owned business located in the Pacific Northwest. The company's collection features cast lead-free pewter findings that are plated in copper, 24-karat gold, and .999 fine silver. Almost all of the products are American made. Check out the website.

Swarovski
www.swarovski.com
I have been a vetted partner with Swarovski for many years. I love using their crystals, and I adore their pearls. If you're buying direct, you have to be ready to buy in big quantities, which is how manufacturers shop. Otherwise, as I mentioned above, you can buy through a retailer like Fire Mountain Gems.

Hord Crystal Corporation
www.hordcrystal.com
Hord Crystal sells to major manufacturers, and you have to order some items wholesale, but their crystal flowers are worth the expense. They often

have sales, so check the website to try some of their beautiful and handmade products.

Tucson Gem and Mineral Show
www.tgms.org/show
This show happens just once a year, but it is the biggest gem show in the world. If you live anywhere in the Tucson, Arizona, area, or if you can somehow make it there, go! It is the whole world coming to you and bringing its best treasures.

Environmental Technology, Inc.
www.eti-usa.com
A few of ETI's products are available only on their website, but big-box stores carry the essentials. ETI keeps adding new, creative items for artists that are American made. They make Castin'Craft® Clear Polyester Casting Resin, EasyMold® Silicone Putty (silicone mold-making putty), resin spray finish, HeatForm™ (thermoplastic sheet), and dyes—all of which are products used throughout this book. I blame them for making me such a big fan of creating molds and colorizing resin.

PART 2:
PROJECTS

A difficulty level is given for each project in this book: Easy, Intermediate, or Advanced. But just because something is labeled Advanced doesn't mean you can't tackle it unless you are an experienced jewelry maker. Advanced projects tend to take more time or are more sensitive, meaning it's harder to get the final result to look clean and pretty due to the skills needed or finicky materials. Read through the instructions before starting a project to decide whether you're ready for it.

"You can have anything you want in life if you dress for it."
— Edith Head

shine

Almost-Instant Molded Pendant

This is a great, fast project to make while trying out interesting new products and pushing them in new directions. If you've never made a mold before, this is an excellent way to learn how to do it. The resin will cure in a matter of minutes, and by adding a few drops of dye, you can make this project truly unique to you.

⚙ **Skill level:** Intermediate

🕐 **Time:** 30 minutes plus necklace assembly time

◎ **Safety notes:** Work in a well-ventilated area; wear gloves; use caution when applying heat

SUPPLIES

◊ Plastic-covered or silicone work surface

◊ Silicone mold-making putty

◊ Disposable gloves

◊ An object to mold

◊ Gold pigment powder (such as mica powder)

◊ Cotton swabs or a small paintbrush

◊ Baby wipes

◊ Casting resin

◊ Red and blue resin dyes

◊ Wooden stir stick

◊ Marker

◊ Disposable measuring cup

◊ Beige thermoplastic sheet

◊ Gold leaf (in sheet form)

◊ Scissors

◊ Heat gun/embossing tool

◊ 2 jump rings

◊ For necklace: chain, beads, jump rings, 20-gauge wire, jewelry pliers, flush cutters

TIP: Thermoplastic sheet is not heat stable, so if you leave it in your hot car, for example, the product will soften again.

1. I have had this Romanesque pin for more than 30 years. Now it's going to make a splendid mold! Wearing gloves and working on a plastic-covered or silicone surface (not paper), mix parts A and B of the putty according to the manufacturer's instructions. Work quickly. After mixing, press the putty to flatten it, then flip it over to make sure it is relatively level.

2. Push the object you want to mold facedown evenly into the putty. Don't jiggle it around or otherwise move it. Let the putty cure for about 10 minutes (or according to the manufacturer's instructions). Remove the item. Your mold is done!

3. Using a small paintbrush or cotton swab, add gold pigment powder where desired in the molded design. Carefully wipe away any excess with a baby wipe.

4. Gather all the resin supplies you will need: casting resin, resin dyes, a wooden stir stick, a marker, and a disposable measuring cup.

5. Wearing gloves, mark the measuring cup for the two equal amounts of the resin you need. Pour in part B, which is clear, and mix in a drop each of the red and blue dyes. Stir well with the stick. You can add another drop or two, but if you dilute the mixture too much, it may not cure correctly.

6. When you are completely ready to start filling in your mold, mix in part A. Be warned: you only have a few minutes before the resin will start to cure, so work swiftly. The warmer the work area is, the faster the resin will cure.

7. Carefully pour the resin into the mold, making sure to fill it to the desired level. While I was making this project, I had other molds prepped to fill with the extra resin, but by the time I was done taking the photos, the resin in the cup had already started to cloud (as you can see in the photo). That meant the curing had started, and it was already too solid to use.

8. See how the resin is blooming into a soft pastel? It is curing while you watch. Mesmerizing! Allow it to cure for about 10 minutes until it is completely solid (or according to the manufacturer's instructions). Then remove your resin cast from the mold.

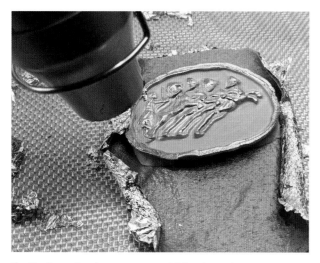

9. Gather the heat gun, gold leaf, and thermoplastic sheet. Cut a piece of thermoplastic sheet a little larger than your new molded object. Lay a small sheet of gold leaf on your work surface and then top it with the thermoplastic sheet. Point the heat gun at the edges of the sheet and start applying heat; the sheet will curl into itself with the gold leaf attached.

10. The idea is to encase the resin piece in a gold frame. Don't try to work fast. Allow the heat to do the work. If the sheet is curling too fast, just back up the heat gun. The resulting pendant will be very lightweight, great for comfortable jewelry. (Ignore the jump rings showing in the photo here; they get added in the next step!)

11. Use two small pieces of thermoplastic sheet to cover half of two jump rings positioned to stick out slightly from the top of the pendant. Prep some small pieces of gold leaf to go on top of the sheet. Using the heat gun, slowly heat the sheet and add the gold leaf to it, smoothing it into the sheet with your fingertips. Let it cool.

12. Your pendant is ready to be attached to a necklace (or anything else you desire). To make this necklace, attach the pendant to several bead links, then attach the bead links to chain using jump rings. Add additional lengths of chain as shown, or create a custom look that pleases you.

Aqua Crystal Drops

This project isn't very hard, but the technique will lead you to almost limitless possibilities once you have mastered it. It basically consists of capturing sparkly bits in resin and then linking them together in whatever arrangement you want.

⚙ **Skill level:** Intermediate

🕐 **Time:** 10 minutes per drop plus curing and necklace assembly time

🛡 **Safety notes:** Work in a well-ventilated area; wear gloves

SUPPLIES

◊ Gold flat acrylic teardrops (with bead holes)

◊ Clear packing tape

◊ Disposable plastic containers

◊ Variety of aqua crystal beads and embellishments

◊ Plastic work surface

◊ Casting resin

◊ Disposable gloves

◊ Wooden stir stick

◊ Marker

◊ Disposable measuring cup

◊ Craft knife

◊ For necklace: 20-gauge brass wire, jump rings, jewelry pliers, flush cutters, vintage chain, gold lobster claw clasp

1. Arrange the teardrops the way you want your necklace to look so that you are sure you are making the right number of crystal drops.

2. If your teardrops have extra holes through them, like mine did, a little ingenuity is required. If you are using solid teardrops, you can skip this step. Cut a piece of packing tape big enough to cover the entire back of the teardrop to seal the holes closed. Then rub every bit of the tape onto the teardrop securely. Trim the tape to make it easier to move the pieces. The tape will be removed at the end.

3. Arrange the teardrops in a disposable container with a flat bottom. Then artistically arrange a mixture of beads and crystals on the surface of each drop. I love a variety of big and small, and a mix of shapes and shades.

4. Gather all the resin supplies you will need: casting resin, a wooden stir stick, a marker, and a disposable measuring cup. Wearing gloves and working on a plastic-protected work surface, mark the measuring cup for the two equal amounts you need. Mix the resin according to the manufacturer's instructions. Remember: You only have a few minutes before the resin will start to cure, so work swiftly.

5. Drop the resin off of the stir stick bit by bit into the center of a teardrop, then move to another teardrop and repeat. Look carefully as the resin spreads out over each teardrop, and go back and add more where needed. The resin must touch each bead and connect with the teardrop. If any resin overflows, don't try to clean it up until it has hardened.

6. Notice how the beads look like they are in water. This is how you know the beads are nicely embedded in the resin and will not come out. Allow the resin to set according to the manufacturer's instructions before trying to pick up any of the drops. Once the resin has fully cured, remove the packing tape (if applicable) and use a craft knife to scrape off any resin drips.

7. Now you can make whatever you desire with your sparkling aqua crystal drops. To make this necklace, arrange the drops and additional beads in your design. Then connect each piece using wire to make bead links. Attach each line of drops and beads to the chain using jump rings, spacing them out evenly.

VARIATIONS

Here is a simplified version of the drops using pearls and the same beads that are used in the Bead Nests Necklace project (see page 139). I can just see a bride wearing this.

This necklace combines glass cobalt beads, 20-gauge silver wire, and silver acrylic teardrops. A variety of AB and non-AB glass beads make it even more interesting.

One of the aqua crystal drops makes a perfect ring when you simply glue it to a ring base using a heavy-duty glue such as E6000. Set the ring upright in floral foam or use painter's tape to secure it until it dries.

VARIATIONS

To create these earrings, drill a hole in the top of the drop and use a jump ring to attach it to the bead above. You could do the same thing to just make a simple drop necklace—easy-peasy but still handmade and stunning!

To coordinate with the necklace, make bangles in three different widths using various Swarovski crystals and some epoxy clay.

After creating the three bangles above, I still had extra epoxy clay mixed. I rolled it into a snake, literally, overlapping the ends and forming a head. I then poked in a few beads all over, including a pair for eyes. I then covered the snake in gold leaf by just pressing one half sheet at a time into the snake. To make this snake, you will want your epoxy clay to already be slightly firm so that it doesn't lose its nice tubular shape; you could not do this with freshly mixed epoxy clay. Voilà, a snake bracelet!

Bead Caps

These bead caps have such an organic feel. They are a great way to use up extra epoxy clay before it hardens so that it doesn't go to waste. Making beads is one way; making bead caps is another. It is so easy to instantly create something so fresh!

 Skill level: Easy

 Time: 10 minutes plus curing time

 Safety notes: Work in a well-ventilated area; wear gloves

SUPPLIES

◊ Epoxy clay

◊ Disposable gloves

◊ Beads

◊ 20-gauge wire

◊ Plastic work surface

◊ Gold leaf

◊ Sealer such as resin spray or clear nail polish

◊ Jewelry pliers

◊ Flush cutters

◊ For earrings: wire, 2 jump rings, 2 pearl drops, 2 eye pins, 2 earring hooks

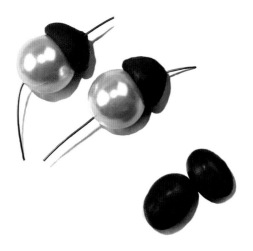

1. Cut 2" (5cm) lengths of wire and thread one through each bead. Wearing gloves, mix the epoxy clay according to the manufacturer's instructions. Roll the clay into small balls or ovals. Slide one ball onto the wire and down onto the top of each bead. Squish it into a little cap on top of the bead, like an acorn.

3. Once the clay has cured (according to the manufacturer's instructions), gently brush off any extra gold leaf crumbs. Seal the caps with a resin spray, clear nail polish, or a brush-on sealer to keep them glorious. Then use them any way you wish! The featured earrings were made with coiled wire, jump rings, and pearl drops on eye pins.

2. Generously wrap small sheets of gold leaf around each clay cap and smooth them down to adhere them. Don't worry about getting gold leaf on the beads.

VARIATIONS

Chunky and misshapen bead caps on larger gems strung onto a thick chain give this necklace a glamorous yet natural feel and keep the proportions intact.

This necklace combines bead caps with bead nests (see page 139) for a super glam, encrusted look.

A series of baroque pearls with a bit of clay showing through combine in a row to create a dynamic pendant that will move as you move.

Beetle Wing Bangle and Ring

To make these super shiny bug bracelets, you can use any blank bangle. Search jewelry and thrift stores for bargain bangles if you enjoy covering over and giving new life to old jewelry. The ring is assembled similarly to the bangle and makes a perfect matching set. Some of the beetle wings may have battle scars and marks from the beetle's life; I appreciate those wings, too. Nature is perfect regardless.

Skill level: Intermediate

Time: 45 minutes for each item plus curing time

Safety notes: Work in a well-ventilated area; wear gloves

SUPPLIES

◊ Wide bangle bracelet

◊ Black epoxy clay

◊ Disposable gloves

◊ Beetle wings (I used jewel wings from the species *Sternocera aequisignata*)

◊ Baby wipes

◊ Scissors

◊ Craft knife

◊ Ring blank

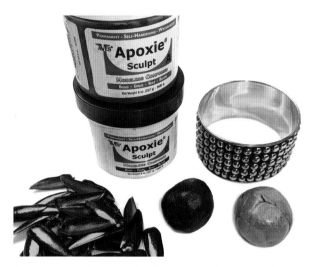

1. Wearing gloves, mix the epoxy clay according to the manufacturer's instructions.

2. Roll the clay into a rope and place it around the bangle. It should go all the way around.

3. Using your fingers and the palm of your hand, spread the clay out to the edges of the bracelet. You can roll it gently on your (plastic-covered) work surface to make it more even. If it seems too soft, just let it set for five to fifteen minutes before shaping.

4. Using a craft knife, trim any excess clay around the edges and press to slightly taper the clay to the edges. This bangle was straight-sided, so the middle is thicker than the edge.

5. Smooth the surface of the clay all around the bangle; it does not have to be perfectly smooth, though. Now it's ready for the wings.

6. Press a row of beetle wings into the clay to embed them. Working row by row, continue adding wings all around the bracelet.

7. See how a little too much clay is poking out here? Before you cut it off, make sure that you smooth all the wings into the clay. Only trim the clay when all of the wings are in place. Then clean the inside of the bracelet and the wings using baby wipes, being careful not to touch the clay with the wipes. Set aside to cure for 24 hours or according to the manufacturer's instructions.

8. Now let's move on to the ring. Grab your ring base, and mix additional clay if you need to.

9. Make a small ball of clay and press it into the ring base to create a mound as shown. Be careful: too little clay and the wings will have nothing to cling to, but too much clay and you could have a mess.

10. Insert the wings with the tips pointing up and the larger base of the wing embedded in the clay. Continue all the way around the ring base.

11. Insert some more wings into the middle. The mound of clay will make the wings in the middle sit higher. Smooth the wings with your fingers just like you would smooth down feathers on a bird, gently and in one direction.

12. Take the last of your clay and make a small snake. Wrap it around the base and tuck it a bit under the ring.

13. Cover the clay with one more row of wings. Overlap the wings if necessary, or trim a wing with scissors to make them all fit. Clean the wings carefully with a baby wipe.

14. If you want to change the color of the ring base band, you can make one last clay snake and press it carefully around the ring band. Don't get any clay on the inside of the band, or it will be scratchy to wear. Set aside to cure for 24 hours or according to the manufacturer's instructions. Now you have a truly stunning set!

VARIATION

For this slightly thinner bangle, trim the wings to fit vertically and alternate their orientation as you embed them. It is truly a statement bracelet. Make a stack of bug wing bangles and watch people's eyes follow them like they are magical—because they are!

Beetle Wing Fingertips

Fancy fingertips are very popular for art photography, but they are also a super choice for those of you wanting to really push your fashion limits! You can wear just one or a whole set on all your fingers. Beetle wings are the perfect size for fingernails. This project is super easy and fast!

Skill level: Easy

Time: 1 hour including drying time

Safety notes: Gloves optional

SUPPLIES

◊ Large metal filigree components

◊ Black nail polish

◊ Disposable gloves (optional)

◊ Straight/chain-nose jewelry pliers

◊ Beetle wings (I used jewel wings from the species *Sternocera aequisignata*)

◊ Scissors

◊ Heavy-duty craft adhesive (such as E6000)

◊ Emerald green flat-backed gems

1. Wearing gloves if desired, paint one side of the component with black polish and let dry. Flip over and repeat. You can always touch up as needed later.

2. Using a pair of chain-nose pliers, grab near the edge of a component at a slight angle and bend the other side down with your fingers. Switch sides with your pliers and repeat to bend the other side down. Make cone shapes so your fingertips will fit into the components securely.

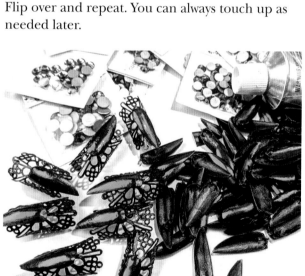

3. Trim any sharp spots off the wings, including the pointy tip, with scissors if desired. Use heavy-duty craft adhesive to glue the wings to the metal, placing the glue on the metal, not the wing, to make less of a mess.

4. Use adhesive to glue on as many flat-backed gems as you like. Again, put the adhesive on the component, not the gem. I used one emerald green gem per fingertip. Wait for the glue to dry and then do any final touchups with the nail polish.

Beetle Wing Necklace

This project allows you to combine beetle wings with glass findings in a creative way. By mixing in jump rings and some gems, you'll tone down the "bugginess" of the wings—but up the glam level at the same time!

⚙ **Skill level:** Intermediate

🕑 **Time:** 2+ hours plus curing time

🛡 **Safety notes:** Work in a well-ventilated area; wear gloves

SUPPLIES

◊ Glass or plastic rings

◊ Black epoxy clay

◊ Disposable gloves

◊ Beetle wings (I used jewel wings from the species *Sternocera aequisignata*)

◊ Assorted flat-backed gems/crystals

◊ Old paintbrush

◊ Baby wipes

◊ Bugs in resin key chain

◊ Large and small jump rings

◊ Chain

◊ Lobster claw clasp

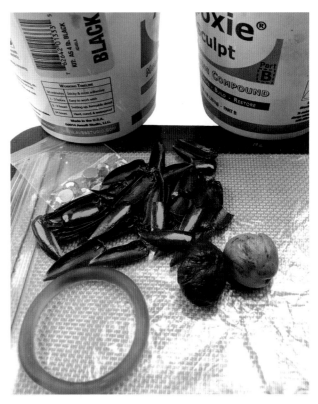

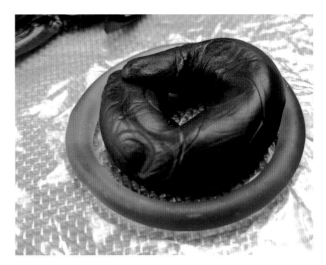

1. Lay out your planned design using the glass rings as markers. You can change things later, but it's good to have an idea of the desired shape before proceeding.

2. Wearing gloves, mix the epoxy clay according to the manufacturer's instructions. Mix enough clay for each circle that you want to make.

3. Roll some clay into a fat snake and coil it in the middle of a ring.

4. Flatten the coil into the ring using your fingers and the palm of your hand. Try to keep it tidy, but it doesn't have to be totally perfect.

5. Before you start putting on the beetle wings, pick the circle up and smooth out the backside. Once you have the wings on it, you will not want to handle it too much.

6. Flip the circle over and fill the front with the wings and gems. Then make holes in the clay large enough for jump rings to be inserted—one, two, or more holes, depending on how you want to use the circle in your necklace assembly. You can use the end of a paintbrush to make the holes. Make them as close to the edges as possible.

7. Clean the ring's edges, gems, and wings with a baby wipe, making sure not to touch the clay with the wipe.

VARIATION

You can also make a simple necklace by just suspending a single buggy circle from a chain.

8. Make the rest of your buggy circles. Allow them to cure for 24 hours or according to the manufacturer's instructions. When all pieces are cured, assemble the necklace using the jump rings, chain, and clasp. Add the resin pendant as a finishing touch.

Beetle Wing Headpiece

This is literally the crowning jewel of the beetle wing projects in this book. People will be drawn to the familiar peacock colors and feathers and then be surprised to see the beetle wings there, too. It's not for the faint of heart—but neither are most of the wow-worthy projects in this book!

 Skill level: Advanced

 Time: 2+ hours plus curing time

 Safety notes: Work in a well-ventilated area; wear gloves

SUPPLIES

◊ Metal headband

◊ 6-gauge black wire

◊ Roofing galvanized tin

◊ Tin snips or old heavy-duty scissors

◊ Heavy-duty craft glue (such as E6000) or clear packing tape

◊ Black epoxy clay

◊ Disposable gloves

◊ Resin sheet (or colorful plastic sheet)

◊ Flat-backed orbs

◊ Colorized crystals (without decoration) (see page 155)

◊ Beetle wings (I used jewel wings from the species *Sternocera aequisignata*)

◊ Bugs

◊ Peacock feathers

◊ Flat-backed gems/crystals

◊ Paint or nail polish

◊ Baby wipes

◊ Black craft paint

2. Using tin snips or old, strong scissors, cut the metal into the shape you want for the headpiece. Here, I have cut chunky strips, folded them over the edge of the headband, and added heavy-duty glue to secure them in place. You could also add a bit of strong clear packing tape to close them.

1. Add a piece of thick wire to the headband to extend it as shown. This will give the support you need for the additional metal pieces. Wrap the wire securely around the headband.

3. Add a small piece of tin to fill the horizontal space and to firm up the shape and provide more surface space to decorate. Before decorating, test the fit and balance of the piece on your head. Then gather your decorative supplies as well as your epoxy clay supplies.

4. Wearing gloves, mix the epoxy clay according to the manufacturer's instructions. Form large ropes of clay and break them into pieces the size of each metal section. Place a rope in each section and work from the center of the clay to press the clay down and out to the edges, covering the metal. Trim off any excess. Repeat for the backside so that the entire form is covered. Smooth all the clay so it is even.

5. It's time to start decorating! Start with the biggest pieces to set up your structure, moving from the center out to the edges. Then fill in with smaller pieces. Cut pieces of the resin/plastic sheet and poke them in near the edges to add a dimensional look. Recolor any bugs that need to match using paint or nail polish. Basically, do your thing!

6. When you're done, tidy up the clay and wipe any clay off of the decorations using baby wipes. Make sure everything is firm and solid, picking the piece up and turning it around. Then allow it to cure for 24 hours or according to the manufacturer's instructions.

7. Once the piece is cured, paint the back black so it blends nicely and has a uniform coating. You could also apply fabric to the back with craft glue. It's time to dance with your new headpiece shining!

Pink and Gold Crown

Since I work with many models with different-sized heads and hairstyles, one-size-fits-all crowns can be problematic. So I came up with a way to make crowns adjustable and as lightweight as possible, yet still stunning. To adjust this crown, you simply twist the wires in the back.

> ⚙ **Skill level:** Advanced
>
> 🕐 **Time:** 2 hours plus curing time
>
> 🛡 **Safety notes:** Work in a well-ventilated area; wear gloves

SUPPLIES

- ◊ Roofing galvanized tin
- ◊ Tin snips or old heavy-duty scissors
- ◊ Marker
- ◊ Small drill bit (³⁄₃₂"/2.4mm) and drill
- ◊ Gold metallic spray paint (primer included, or prime separately)
- ◊ Gold wire
- ◊ Bronze epoxy clay
- ◊ Disposable gloves
- ◊ Gold leaf
- ◊ Metallic embellishments
- ◊ Pink embellishments
- ◊ Baby wipes
- ◊ Jewelry pliers
- ◊ Flush cutters
- ◊ Craft knife
- ◊ Old paintbrush

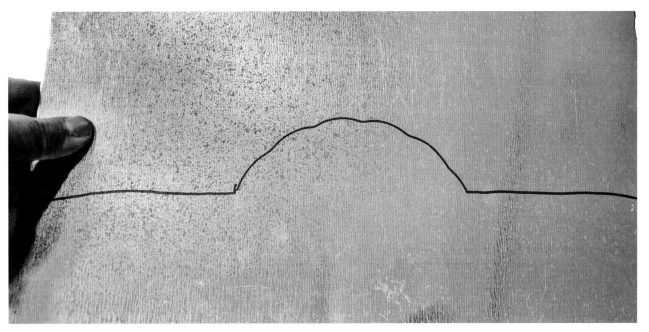

1. Measure the front of your head from ear to ear. Draw the desired crown shape on the tin to the correct length and use tin snips to cut it out, making sure to remove any sharp edges.

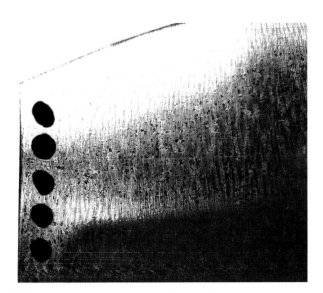

2. Use a marker to draw a line of drill holes along each side of the crown, as evenly spaced as possible, then drill them.

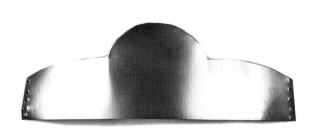

3. Use gold spray paint to cover the metal on both sides, allowing it to dry between coats. Use a primer if possible.

4. Lay out embellishments on the metal in your desired design to get an idea of placement before proceeding.

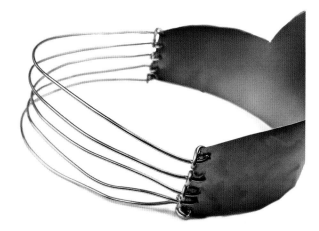

5. Cut pieces of wire at least 4" (10cm) longer than will be needed to make the crown fit around your head. Lace the wires through the holes. Pinch the ends of the wires closed with your fingers.

6. Fold each wire's end over and around itself to secure the wire to the crown. Trim off any extra wire and make sure the ends are bent so that they will not scratch your head. Don't make a big wire knot at each wire end; the wire will be covered in epoxy clay later, and you don't want big blobs on the sides of the crown.

7. Wearing gloves, mix the epoxy clay according to the manufacturer's instructions. You can mix up a batch about the size of an apple to start; make more if needed. Roll the clay into a long, fat snake and place it on the crown. Flatten it as you go, section by section, so it covers the entire front of the crown.

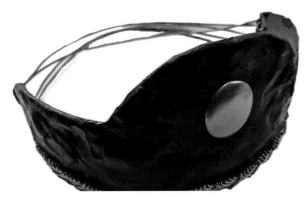

8. Smooth out all of the clay until it is even. You can remove your gloves at this point to make it easier to work with the embellishments. Start adding the decorations, making sure that you push each item securely into the clay.

9. This is the assembled crown before applying gold leaf. Make any final adjustments to the embedded items now.

11. Apply gold leaf to the front of the crown, cutting sheets in half and working them into the clay with your fingers. Add gold to all of the clay. The less you push on the gold leaf, the fewer cracks will form on it. You can use a brush to push the leaf into small areas. Once you're done, use baby wipes to gently clean the gold off the decorations. The final cleaning will be done later.

10. Make sure you've covered the wire ends with clay. Then clean off any excess clay on the backside of the crown with a craft knife. Wipe the back of the crown clean with baby wipes, being careful not to touch the clay with the wipes.

12. Your head is an oval; use something solid to help the crown hold an oval shape while it dries. Allow the clay to cure for 24 hours. Then, using an old paintbrush, wipe off any gold crumbs. Your crown is now ready to wear and enjoy!

Beaded Cuff

This project is chock full of beautiful beads. For the integrity of the bracelet, try to use only one wire, as directed, to keep the wire knots to a minimum.

Skill level: Intermediate

Time: 1 hour

Safety notes: None

SUPPLIES

◊ Beads

◊ 22-gauge wire

◊ Bracelet frame

◊ Round-nose jewelry pliers

◊ Flush cutters

1. Collect your beads for the project. How many beads depends on how big your beads are, if you want to overlap strands, etc. This particular frame provides about 10 square inches (64 square centimeters) of beading space. If you are using small beads, think about how many times you have to wrap it, and multiply that by how many beads it takes to do one wrap. String all the beads you think you want to use onto the wire without cutting the wire from the spool. Err on the side of more beads.

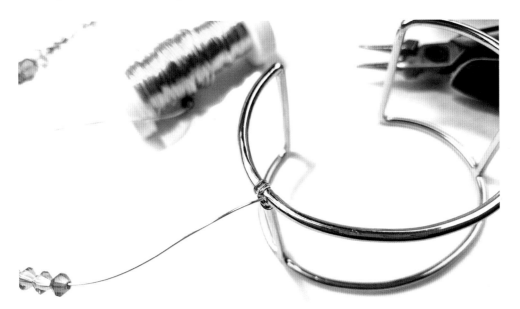

2. Tie the beaded wire at a T junction so it doesn't slide around. Wrap the wire around a few times, pulling it tight and adding a half knot. Do not cut the wire off the spool yet! That will be done at the very end.

3. Trim the extra wire on the knot, leaving less than ¼" (0.5cm), and tuck it into the knot so that it won't scratch or come undone. Then start pushing beads forward all the way up to the knot and bracelet.

4. It's time to start wrapping beads onto the frame. For this bracelet, we're going to wrap beads in one direction, then wrap empty wire back toward the starting point to finish wrapping beads on the last section. As you wrap each row, make sure none of the beads sneak onto the backside.

5. As you work, position the beads so they fit nicely between the edges of the frame, or, if the beads are larger, let them bulge up slightly. You are in control of your end product. If you want a bracelet that is very thick with beads, you can wrap strands of beads over each other during this part or closer to the end. Work all the way to the far end of the bracelet.

7. Wrap all the way back to the starting point using bare wire, then wrap beads over the remaining section as you did originally. Note how the wire is visible in diagonal lines on the back, as I have repeatedly gone over the other side to make my way back to the empty portion of the bracelet. At the end, you will make this extra wire almost disappear, so don't worry.

6. At this point you will have wrapped roughly three quarters of the bracelet and it is time to make your way back to the empty portion by wrapping wire only, no beads. It will seem like a lot of wire, but don't worry; at the end you will gently push the wire in so it disappears under the beads.

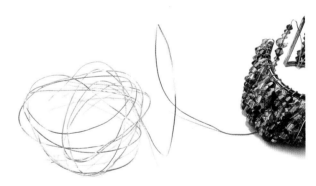

8. It's finally time to cut the wire. Give yourself plenty of wire to work with before you cut it—at least 24" (61cm). You will use this wire much like thread to secure the beads onto the frame so they don't move around. If you realize you cut your wire too short, add more wire by tying a second knot. But the fewer knots you make, the cleaner your final product will be.

10. Make a small knot where you come to a stop with the whipstitch. Your wire under the beads will look something like this. The final step is to give each of the wire strands on the underside of the bracelet a tiny twist with your round-nose pliers. This step is important, as it tightens the wire slightly and makes all of the wire more uniform.

9. To secure the beads, work first on one side of an end and then the other side. Loop the remaining wire around the frame like a sewing whipstitch. You are just whipstitching the wire between the beaded wire for about 1" (2.5cm) on each side. The weak parts of the cuff are these ends, as you don't want the beads to slip off the frame. Use your fingers to see if there is any looseness. Double-check that you have a firm enough end before you work your wire to the other side to do the whipstitch there.

11. Push any wires that are visible on the outside behind and underneath the beads where possible. They will become almost invisible as they are moved behind the beads. Give them a tiny twist from the backside as needed, too.

Gem Windows

This project creates jewelry that is almost like stained glass using real gems. You can put anything into this project. It is perfect for when you want to enjoy seeing the front and back of an item. The key is the findings: you can use any kind or shape, but they must be completely solid, with no breaks, because the UV resin will seep through even the tiniest crack.

⚙ **Skill level:** Advanced

🕑 **Time:** 1 hour plus curing time

🛡 **Safety notes:** Gloves optional

SUPPLIES

◊ Metal hoops

◊ Clear packing tape

◊ Scissors

◊ Findings/gemstones with no cracks or gaps

◊ UV resin

◊ Disposable gloves (optional)

◊ UV light or direct sunlight

◊ Floral foam

◊ Adhesive remover (such as Goo Gone)

◊ Paper towels

◊ Small drill bit (³⁄₃₂"/2.4mm) and drill

◊ Jump rings

◊ Chain

◊ Clasp

◊ Jewelry pliers

◊ Flush cutters

1. Create a workspace made with white cardstock slipped into zip-top plastic bags. Set these sheets on a tray. This will make moving things later much easier.

2. Cut clear tape pieces at least ½" (1.3cm) larger than the metal hoops and adhere them to the hoops. The tape side will be the backside. Press down on the hoop as firmly as you can, making sure that the tape is totally, completely attached all the way around. If you skimp on this step, the resin will make a mess. Note: Don't touch the tape inside the circle, as it will leave fingerprints on your project.

3. Once the tape is sealed to the circles, place them on the prepared workspace. Pieces of tape will try to stick to other pieces, so give them space.

4. Add gemstones to each circle, balancing the colors. Leave a little bit of empty space on either side of each circle to drill small holes later to link them together.

5. Drip UV resin onto each hoop of stones slowly, doing just one small area at a time and allowing it to flow into the areas around the stones. Don't drip it on top of the stones or hoop. Let the resin slowly spread. You can wear gloves for this process if you want, but they tend to get caught in the tape, so I don't wear them. If you skip the gloves, wash your hands after working with the UV resin.

6. Make sure you use enough resin to connect the gems to the circle and bond the stones together, but don't over fill. If you get any resin where it shouldn't be, remove it with a craft knife after the resin has cured; immediately after it has cured, it is still easy to remove. When you are done adding resin, cure the pieces under a UV light or in direct sunlight. UV resin cures in 20 minutes with any UV light.

7. Once the resin has cured, peel off the tape from the backs of the pieces. Wearing gloves if desired, use paper towels and an adhesive remover to remove any traces of the adhesive. Wash the pieces in hot, soapy water and dry them. If you also want to make the backs look like glass, push the front sides down levelly into floral foam and add more UV resin to the backs, just inside the hoops' edges. Cure in UV light again.

8. These are the finished backsides. They are shiny and translucent. Now, drill small holes in the pieces, one on either side for connectors or just one for pendants.

9. Connect the circles with jump rings, lengths of chain, and a clasp as shown. I added a dangle at the end of the chain here, which adds a weighted, sparkly flourish.

10. I made the largest piece into a pendant, adding a matching bead on top, a larger jump ring, and a chain.

VARIATION

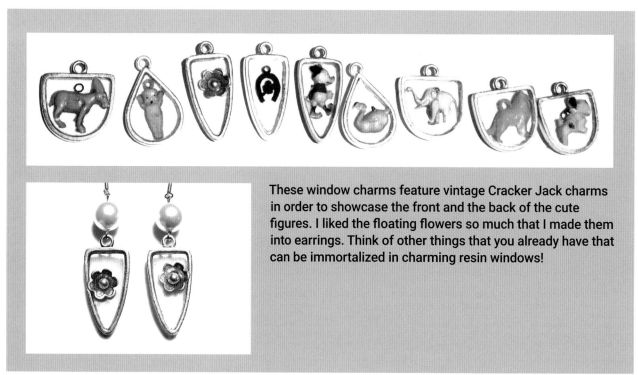

These window charms feature vintage Cracker Jack charms in order to showcase the front and the back of the cute figures. I liked the floating flowers so much that I made them into earrings. Think of other things that you already have that can be immortalized in charming resin windows!

Boho Earrings

It is great to have big earrings back in fashion. Making large, dramatic, and yet lightweight earrings is really fun. And you hardly need any supplies to make these! Note: This project is not good for people who have highly sensitive earlobes or ear-piercing allergies.

 Skill level: Intermediate

 Time: 30 minutes plus curing time

 Safety notes: Work in a well-ventilated area; wear gloves

SUPPLIES

◊ 6-gauge gold wire

◊ 22-gauge brass wire

◊ Bronze epoxy clay

◊ Disposable gloves

◊ Loose rhinestones

◊ Gold pigment powder (such as mica powder)

◊ Cotton swab

◊ Jewelry pliers

◊ Flush cutters

◊ Earring backs

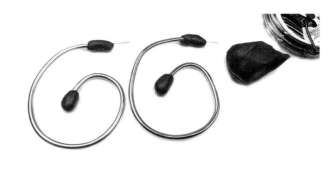

1. Cut two pieces of 6-gauge wire about 8" (20cm) long. Bend them into matching curls.

2. Wearing gloves, mix a small about of epoxy clay according to the manufacturer's instructions. Add a ball on each end of each earring. Slip a 2" (5cm) piece of 22-gauge wire securely into the clay on the outer end of each earring. This will become the earring post to go with the earring back. You can trim it later as needed.

3. Remove your gloves so you can easily work with the small stones. Press stones into the clay to evenly cover all of it.

4. Using a cotton swab, apply a generous amount of pigment powder to the clay. It will adhere perfectly. Let the clay cure for 24 hours. Wipe off the excess pigment powder. Use an earring back to finish your stunning new pair of earrings.

High-Shine Headband

A combination of thermoplastic sheet and epoxy clay keeps this headband lightweight. I always think about comfort, especially when I am creating something that a little girl might wear. It is easy and fun to "paint" with eye shadow on the thermoplastic sheet. When you apply heat, the colors bond to the sheet and become permanent.

⚙️ **Skill level:** Advanced

🕐 **Time:** 1 hour plus curing time

🛡️ **Safety notes:** Work in a well-ventilated area; wear gloves; use caution when applying heat

SUPPLIES

◊ Metal headband

◊ Beige thermoplastic sheet

◊ Marker

◊ Scissors

◊ Craft heat gun/embossing tool

◊ Pigment powders (such as mica powder) and/or eye shadows

◊ Cotton swabs

◊ 20-gauge wire

◊ Flush cutters

◊ Gold leaf

◊ Red, blue, and white epoxy clay

◊ Disposable gloves

◊ Flat-backed gems and crystals

◊ Baby wipes

◊ Old paintbrush

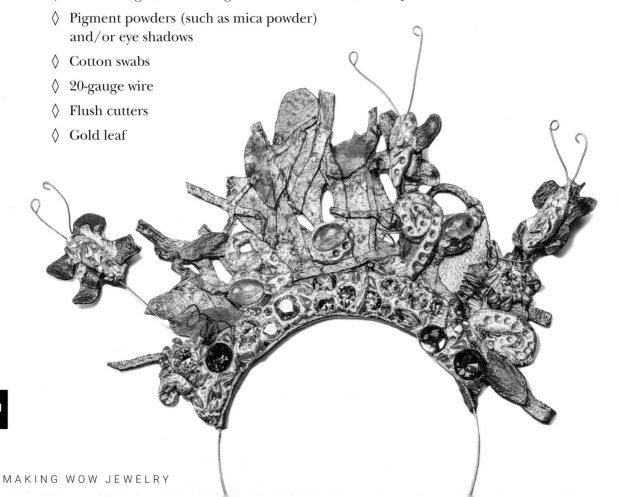

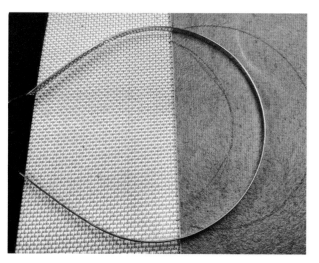

1. Place the headband on the thermoplastic sheet and draw an arch below and above it. Cut this shape out.

2. Cut darts in the bottom arch as shown.

3. Apply heat to the darts using the heat gun, just until they start to shrink. Watch carefully, as it happens very quickly. Before they cool, fold the darts up around the headband and stick them to the upper arch.

4. While the main part is cooling, cut a bunch of strips, leaf shapes, flower shapes, and butterflies from the thermoplastic sheet. Lay out the cut pieces on top of the main part so they all touch each other, creating a weblike form; this will help keep the structure strong.

5. Just like painting, use pigment powders and/ or eye shadows to color the pieces, applying the colors with cotton swabs. Use green on the leaves, pinks and purples on the flowers, and gold and bronze as highlights and accents for richness. Color the butterflies as well, but don't place them on the structure—set them aside for later.

6. Using the heat gun, apply just enough heat to bond the pieces together. They will slightly shrink. If you hold the heat gun too close, the foam will start to curl. Pull back the heat and re-flatten with your fingers. Heat the butterflies separately just to bond the color to them.

7. While the main piece cools, work on the butterflies. Start by creating small springs by firmly wrapping 20-gauge wire around a marker. Include some extra unwrapped length on one end to lay down the length of the butterfly and more unwrapped length on the other end to stick into the epoxy clay later.

8. Lay the wire onto the butterfly's body.

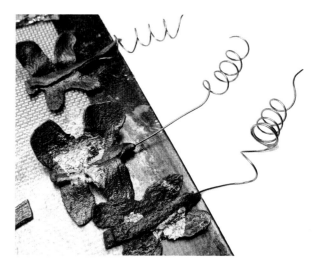

9. Cover the wire with a piece of thermoplastic sheet that has been colorized with powders.

10. Using the heat gun, gently melt the sheet so the wire is bonded inside the body. While the butterflies are still warm, add a few small snippets of gold leaf and adjust any powders to make them bolder or more reflective.

11. Wearing gloves, mix a batch of lavender epoxy clay according to the manufacturer's instructions. Use equal parts of red, blue, and white, referring to a color mixing chart if necessary (such as the one here: *www.avesstudio.com/12_color_chart_pantone.pdf*).

12. Roll the clay into a long snake. Set aside some of the clay to adhere individual stones and create fiddleheads on the headband later.

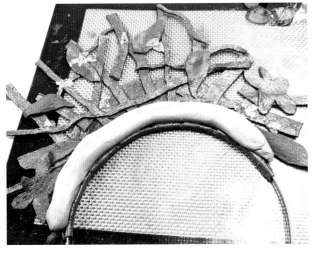

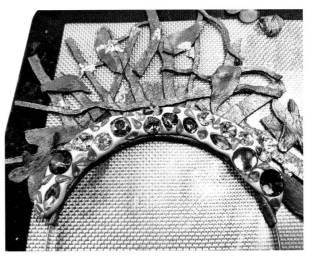

13. Place the clay rope on the base of the headband, on top of the thermoplastic sheet, as shown.

14. Press stones into the clay. Stick the butterflies' wires into the clay, making sure that they are totally secure. When the clay cures, the springy wire will allow them to wiggle!

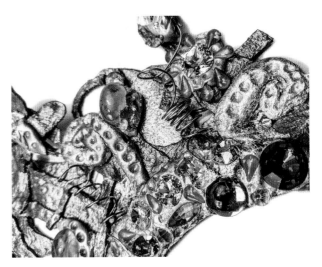

15. Once you are happy with the stones, add pieces of gold leaf to the clay. It helps to use a paintbrush to slightly push it in. Use the rest of the clay to add dimensional items like fiddleheads (visible in the next photo). Apply additional stones by using small bits of clay like an adhesive. Add texture by using any tool, like a pencil point, to poke the clay.

16. Add any additional pigment powders and texture one last time to different clay areas for more depth and warmth. Use baby wipes to do a final cleanup of any clay on top of the gems. Allow the headband to cure for 24 hours or according to the manufacturer's instructions. You now have a masterpiece!

Super-Shiny Dangle Necklace

You can create completely custom decorative dangles that are as shiny as they are stunning. This technique is only difficult because it does take practice to get the shapes right and the silver leaf smooth. Have fun coloring anything, including names, logos, fabric, or whatever inspires you. The silver will make the marker art glow, and the sealer will ensure you can wear it forever.

⚙️ **Skill level:** Advanced

🕓 **Time:** 3 hours

🛡️ **Safety notes:** Work in a well-ventilated area; use caution when applying heat

SUPPLIES

◊ 12-gauge aluminum wire

◊ Flush cutters

◊ Beige thermoplastic sheet

◊ Markers

◊ Scissors

◊ Craft heat gun/embossing tool

◊ Silver leaf

◊ Sealing spray

◊ Rhinestones and embellishments

◊ Heavy-duty craft glue (such as E6000)

◊ Small drill bit (³⁄₃₂"/2.4mm) and drill

◊ Jump rings

◊ Chain

◊ Lobster clasp

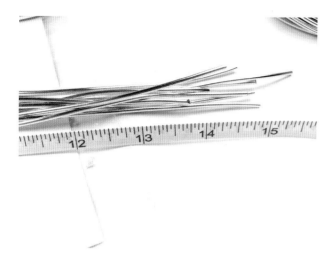

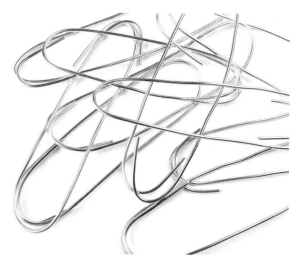

1. Decide on the shape you want to make the dangles; I went with long ovals. Cut eight wires of the same length, about 14" (35cm) each, and one wire that is 2" (5cm) longer. The longest piece will become the middle dangle of the necklace.

2. Create an oval with each wire, but do not knot the ovals closed. Just overlap the ends a bit.

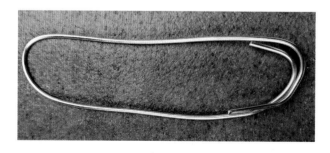

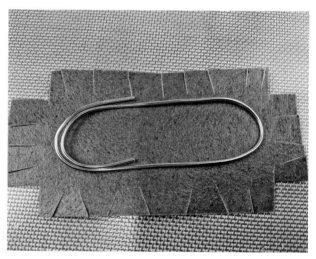

3. Place the shiny side of the thermoplastic sheet face down with the wire oval on top. Use a marker to outline the oval with about a ½" (1.3cm) margin. Set the wire oval aside and cut the oval shape out of the thermoplastic sheet, with either square corners or rounded corners.

4. Cut small slits all the way around the sheet and notch out the corners if desired to remove some of the bulk. Be careful not to cut into the main area. Place the wire oval back on top of the sheet.

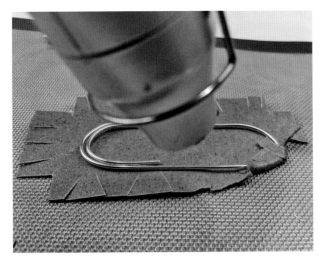

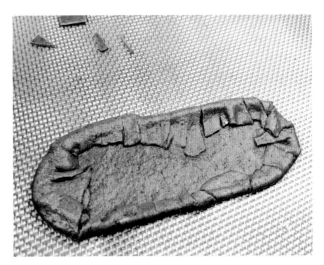

5. Using the heat gun, apply heat to one corner of the sheet. As the sheet heats up, remove the heat gun and fold the notched edges up and around the wire oval, pressing them into the rest of the sheet until they stick.

6. Reapply heat in a new area and continue this way to fold over all the notched edges. Press the edges in toward the center and make sure all of the wire is covered. This will be the backside of the dangle.

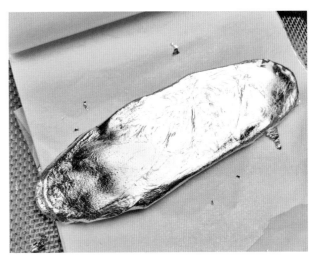

7. Add a little more heat to warm the entire dangle. Then place it, smooth side down, on top of a sheet of silver leaf. Smooth the leaf onto the thermoplastic sheet. It should instantly adhere and bond. If it doesn't, add a little more heat. Wrap more silver leaf around to cover the entire dangle on both sides, smoothing it down.

8. This is the smooth, shiny side of the dangle. This will be the front.

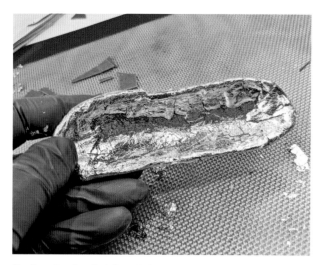

9. On the backside of the dangle, push and drag your finger into the center to bow the dangle out into a concave shape. By pushing from underneath, while the thermoplastic sheet is warm, you can easily create this dimension. Or skip this step if you would like a flat, smooth front.

10. Make the rest of the dangles. When you have finished them all, it's time to decorate! Use colored markers to draw directly on the silver leaf. You can also use nail polish. Layer on lots of color or let the silver shine through. It's your art statement!

11. Spray all of the finished pieces with a sealing spray.

12. Using heavy-duty craft glue to adhere rhinestones to the dangles as desired.

VARIATIONS

This single dangle makes a statement on its matching chunky chain.

These marker art earrings are super lightweight and comfortable. All you need is a few jump rings and earring hooks.

13. Drill small holes in the top of each dangle with a drill. Add the dangles to a chain using jump rings, spacing them so the shorter ones are on the sides and the largest central dangle is in the middle. Finish the back of the chain with a lobster clasp.

Thermoplastic Cuff Collection

This collection of five different bangles will give you a great idea of just how flexible and fun thermoplastic sheet can be. From markers to gems to intricate weaving patterns, there are are a lot of things you can incorporate into these bracelets.

 Skill level: Intermediate

 Time: 30 minutes to 1 hour per bracelet

 Safety notes: Work in a well-ventilated area; use caution when applying heat

SUPPLIES

- ◊ Bangle bracelet base
- ◊ Beige and black thermoplastic sheet
- ◊ Black marker
- ◊ Scissors
- ◊ Craft heat gun/embossing tool
- ◊ Silver leaf
- ◊ Colorful markers
- ◊ Rhinestones and embellishments
- ◊ Metal charms
- ◊ Pigment powders (such as mica powder) and/or eye shadows
- ◊ Cotton swabs or small paintbrush
- ◊ Tape
- ◊ Sealing spray

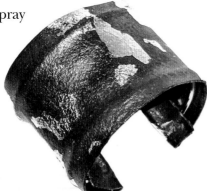

CUFF 1: MARKER SHINE

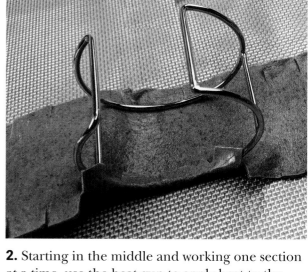

1. Measure the bracelet frame and cut a piece of thermoplastic sheet so it is larger than the frame on all sides. Cut darts in the sheet and notch out the corners to remove bulk.

2. Starting in the middle and working one section at a time, use the heat gun to apply heat to the sheet. As the sheet heats up, remove the heat and fold the notched edges up and around the wire, pressing them into the rest of the sheet until they stick. The sheet should not be uncomfortably hot to the touch; if it is, let it cool slightly. You can always reheat it.

3. Once the sides are folded and secure, gently heat one end of the sheet at a time and fold the tabs over the frame.

4. Apply heat as necessary to neaten any overly bulky areas. You can carefully trim excess with a craft knife or scissors.

5. Working on a paper or plastic surface, spread out the silver leaf you want to use. You can work directly on the paper of the silver leaf pad.

6. Slowly heat the front side of the bracelet, one section at a time, and place the silver leaf on it. Cover the entire front of the bracelet. The silver leaf will adhere to the warm sheet. Gently heat the back of the bracelet and add more leaf. Once the bracelet is totally covered in leaf, use a brush to dust off any silver crumbs.

7. Now it's time to color with permanent markers! You could match a fabric, have your child create a painting, trace a logo, write your name, or draw anything you want. Double-check that the edges of the bracelet are colored, too. Place your bracelet on a plastic bag to make sure you don't smear any marker onto your work surface.

8. Seal the bracelet with a sealing spray. It is art for your wrist!

CUFF 2: COLORFUL POWDERS

1. Cut a piece of thermoplastic sheet that is 1" (2.5cm) longer and 1" (2.5cm) wider than the bracelet frame; do not notch the edges. Slowly heat the sheet to activate it. Add bits of metal leaf in copper, silver, and gold. Add pigment powders and/or eye shadows. Allow the sheet to cool.

2. Lay the colored sheet on top of the bracelet frame. Apply heat to the center with the heat gun, allowing the sheet to slump onto the frame. Continue applying heat to both sides, curling the sheet around the frame. Go slowly. Fold the ends around the frame by using a short blast of heat and pressing it onto itself to secure the ends. Once the piece is cool, spray it with a sealing spray.

CUFF 3: METAL ACCENTS

1. Using the same method shown in Cuff 1: Marker Shine, completely cover the bracelet frame with thermoplastic sheet.

2. Cut a long, thin strip of thermoplastic sheet and lace it through the metal charms you want to use—in this case, beetles. Lay the strung charms on the bracelet. Starting in the middle, slowly and gently heat a section of the strip at a time and press it down to adhere it to the cuff. Work with your fingers from the backside to push up while your other hand pushes down in order to keep the cuff's smooth shape.

3. While the cuff is still warm, brush gold pigment powder all over it. Spray with a sealing spray.

CUFF 4: STUDDED STONES

1. Cut a piece of thermoplastic sheet slightly larger than the bracelet frame; don't cut darts. Place gemstones on the sheet (but not near the edges), and heat it gently with the heat gun. Press the stones into the sheet. You can turn it over and press the sheet around the stones from the backside. Some stones will fall off, so start with a few extra, and repeat as necessary. Allow it to cool to check how well the stones are embedded.

2. Place the gem-studded sheet on top of the bracelet frame. Start to heat it in the middle so it slumps over the frame. Slowly curl the sheet around the frame as it softens, only wrapping the ends around the frame to secure them. Add a touch of gold pigment powder for highlights while the sheet is still warm. Create a slight ruffle with the edges, and then allow the bracelet to cool completely.

CUFF 5: WOVEN LATTICE

1. Cut five strips of thermoplastic sheet that are about 2" (5cm) longer than the bracelet frame. Cut about ten strips that are about 1" (2.5cm) longer than the bracelet width. Tape the long strips to one of the short strips as shown. Now you are ready to start weaving.

2. Weave the short strips through the long strips one at a time. Tape the far end once the lattice is finished so it won't fall apart when you pick it up.

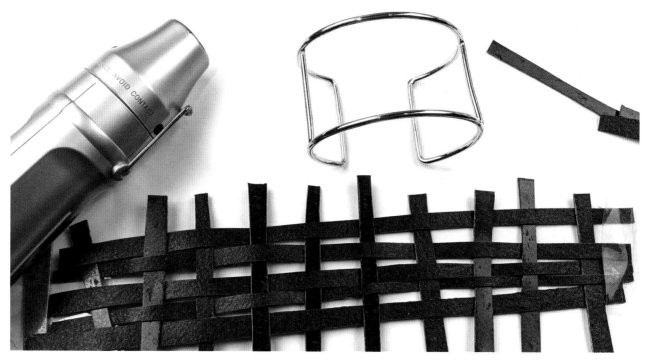

3. Pick up the lattice and place it on top of the bracelet frame. Using a heat gun, gently and evenly start heating the sheet in the center of the lattice. Allow it to gently slump over one side of the frame. Go slowly. Back off the heat if it starts to curl. Wrap the woven ends around the cuff's frame to secure the lattice to the bracelet. Repeat along the other side.

4. Trim off the ends where the tape is once the lattice is mostly secured to the frame. Fold the ends as you gently heat each strip. Allow everything to bond by pressing on the strips as they touch themselves. Add extra strips to fill in any areas where you want more coverage.

5. While the piece is still warm, brush on pigment powders or eye shadows, which will adhere to the warm sheet. Allow the bracelet to cool completely. Apply a sealing spray to finish it.

Magnetic Clasp

I always had problems finding necklace backs that allow for many strands, so I started making them myself. I love to hear the clicking sound as the magnetic halves snap together. These magnets really are strong. Just make sure that the magnets are oriented correctly to attract each other. This version is an embellished clasp, but you could also omit the add-ons and just stick with gold leaf.

⚙ **Skill level:** Advanced

🕐 **Time:** 1 hour plus curing time

🛡 **Safety notes:** Work in a well-ventilated area; wear gloves

SUPPLIES

◊ Bronze epoxy clay

◊ Disposable gloves

◊ 2 five-strand necklace separators

◊ Marker

◊ 2 pairs of super strong, rare earth, round, disc magnets (10mm x 3mm)

◊ Craft knife

◊ Gold leaf

◊ Metal leaves

◊ Tiny metal balls

◊ Old paintbrush

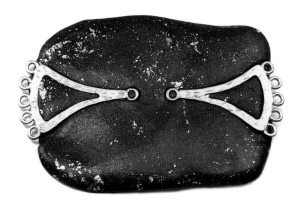

1. To create two equal pieces for a magnetic clasp like this, it is easier to start with one piece and cut it in two. Mix a batch of epoxy clay according to the manufacturer's instructions. Flatten a piece of clay and press the separators on top as shown, with the ends sticking out.

TOP   Bottom

3. Make sure that the loops for the separators are not covered in clay. Trim the clay along to the sides to remove some of the bulk away from the looped edge.

2. Mark your work surface TOP and BOTTOM either by drawing directly on the plastic or by adding a paper note. This marking is essential to make sure you place the magnets correctly. Cover the separators with a little bit of clay, and make sure the clay is smoothed out. Then cut the piece in half, separating the halves.

5. Add gold leaf to one section on the magnet side only, and all over the other piece.

4. Pair two magnets together. As you separate them, place them facing each other into the TOP and BOTTOM pieces of clay. Press them in, but don't press them so deep that they won't be able to connect when the clasp is in use. If you need to practice or check to make sure you have them correctly placed, do it now. Repeat with another pair of magnets.

6. Insert metal leaves into the top (non-magnet) side of the less-covered section and the magnet side of the other section. Keep in mind how the clasp will come together at the end, and decide on the direction of your leaves accordingly. If you need to visually test the fit, do it without letting the magnets come together, as they will pull right out of the soft clay.

7. Push tiny balls into the clay between the metal leaves where you still see clay exposed. Make sure they are evenly spaced around the leaves. When I made this clasp, I decided after the fact that I wanted to add balls to the other half as well, which I did with UV resin.

8. Push gold leaf with a paintbrush into the remaining areas on the top of the ball-covered piece so it can adhere to the clay. Double-check that all the edges of both pieces are covered in gold leaf and everything is securely embedded in the clay. Do not let the magnets get near each other during this process. Let the clay firm up for two hours.

9. After waiting two hours, place the two pieces together so that the magnets click. Slightly shift and press them together so they perfectly match. Don't try to pull them apart at this point, as the magnets will still pull out of the clay. Allow the clasp to cure together for 24 hours or as directed in the manufacturer's instructions.

10. You can use this finished clasp to create a five-strand pearl necklace like this, or whatever other five-strand creation you desire.

Mosaic Necklace

I cherish the collection of micro mosaic picture frames that I bought on a trip to Italy while I was in college. Later in life, I found that there were plenty of vintage mosaic jewelry pieces at reasonable prices available on eBay, and I couldn't resist buying some. Look what you can do with them! I like using them with these clear frames so you can see the flip side and the little "Made in Italy" stamps.

⚙ **Skill level:** Intermediate

🕐 **Time:** 1 hour plus curing time

🛡 **Safety notes:** Gloves optional

SUPPLIES

- ◊ Vintage mosaic jewelry
- ◊ Jewelry pliers
- ◊ Flush cutters
- ◊ Mini clear plastic frames
- ◊ Clear packing tape
- ◊ UV resin
- ◊ Disposable gloves (optional)
- ◊ UV light or direct sunlight
- ◊ Adhesive remover (such as Goo Gone)
- ◊ Paper towels
- ◊ Small drill bit (³⁄₃₂"/2.4mm) and drill
- ◊ Jump rings
- ◊ Chain
- ◊ Lobster clasp

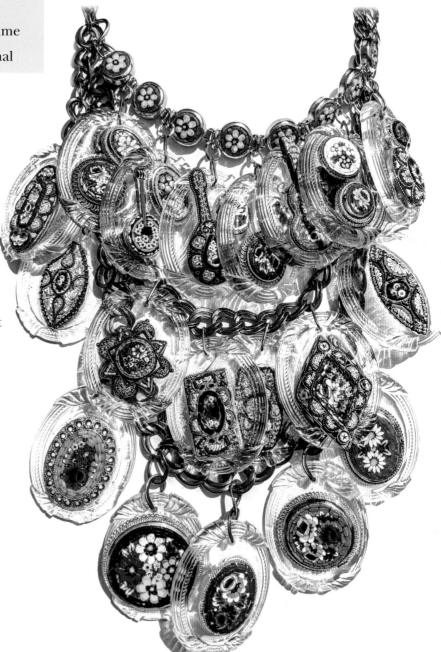

2. Using flush cutters, remove all of the jewelry parts from the pieces so each mosaic item can lay flat.

1. Collect the mosaic pieces you want to use for this project. In general, they should be small enough to fit inside the plastic frames you have.

3. These particular clear plastic frames have holes in them. To keep the resin inside the frame, cut pieces of packing tape and burnish them really well onto the backside of the frame. Push hard as you rub them on the table so they are totally stuck all the way around. The tape will be removed later.

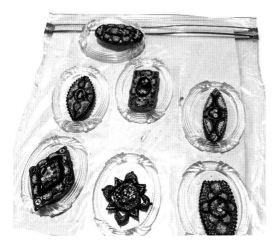

4. Set the mosaic pieces onto the frames as desired. Move the pieces to a plastic-covered, portable setup like the one described on page 94. Wearing gloves if desired, add UV resin to each frame until the mosaic pieces are sitting in a pool of resin, but not so much resin that the frame overflows. Don't drip resin onto the mosaic pieces themselves; see page 95 for more details on how to use UV resin effectively. If you don't wear gloves, wash your hands after working with the UV resin.

6. Use jump rings to attach each frame to the chain.

5. Cure the pieces in sunlight or under a UV light. UV resin cures in 20 minutes with any UV light. Once totally cured, remove the tape from the backsides. If there is any stickiness left from the tape, clean it off with an adhesive remover and paper towels. Drill a hole through the top of each frame for a jump ring to hold it to the chain.

7. I used a whole mosaic bracelet with chain along the back instead of a plain chain for the top section of my necklace.

8. Creating this three-tiered necklace is as simple as taking three separate necklace strands and combining them with jump rings.

VARIATION

Create an epoxy clay bangle bracelet by following the process described on page 66. Add gold leaf and then press in the mosaic jewelry components, trimmed free of pins and any other backings, pushing them flat into the bangle.

Lavender and Gold Drop Necklace

Creating a necklace that is all about purple was my goal here. Super-soft lavender epoxy clay is easy to blend using a color chart. With it, you can make your own beads in all kinds of shapes, including tubes and squished forms with a stone stuck in the middle. Gold leaf tops it all off for a truly glitzy effect.

> ⚙️ **Skill level:** Advanced
>
> ⏱️ **Time:** 2 hours plus curing time
>
> 🛡️ **Safety notes:** Work in a well-ventilated area; wear gloves

SUPPLIES

◊ Red, blue, and white epoxy clay

◊ Disposable gloves

◊ Plastic work surface

◊ Gold leaf

◊ Small AB flat-backed gems, beads, and embellishments in light amethyst shades

◊ Baby wipes

◊ Oval jump rings

◊ Jump rings

◊ Chain

◊ S-hook clasp

◊ 20-gauge brass wire

◊ Head pins

◊ Jewelry pliers

◊ Flush cutters

5. Repeat steps 3 and 4 to make other logs and shapes, inserting oval jump rings into the ends only. Make sure that the rings are embedded well in the clay.

6. Use up any extra clay by creating beads or covering other objects, like these plastic components I'm using here. I'll make them into earrings. Cover the items in more gold leaf.

7. Add embellishments and create elongated beads using the clay, crystals, and gold leaf. Make sure that you are creating holes for jump rings where needed. When you are done embellishing, gently clean off any clay from the stones with baby wipes.

8. Allow the clay to completely harden overnight. Using an old paintbrush, sweep off any gold crumbs until all of the excess is removed. You should see some of the lavender clay peeking through the gold.

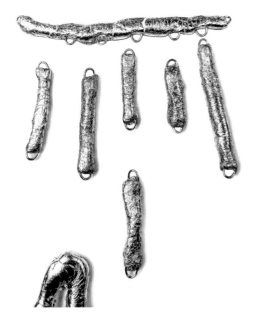

9. Lay out the components that you have created before you start connecting them. Look for interest and balance.

10. Connect everything with jump rings so that each part can move. Use wire and eye pins as needed to create and add bead links. Add the chain and your closure using jump rings.

11. This necklace is now ready for its beauty shot! I just love it. Check out the matching earrings I made using extra clay, too.

VARIATION

This pair of bracelets was created by mixing a pink epoxy clay to match the pink pearls. An area of gold leaf on one of the bracelets adds interest.

Beaded Wire Crown

I have been creating wiggly wire crowns forever using all colors of wire and adding all kinds of beads, feathers, organics, etc. I just love the endless possibilities. The key to this crown is that it is only made of two wires: one to make the crown and one to add the beads. This increases the firmness and integrity of the finished product. Make one and you will be hooked!

⚙️ **Skill level:** Intermediate

🕐 **Time:** 1 hour

🛡️ **Safety notes:** None

SUPPLIES

◊ 12-gauge gold wire

◊ 24-gauge gold wire

◊ Jewelry pliers

◊ Flush cutters

◊ Beads

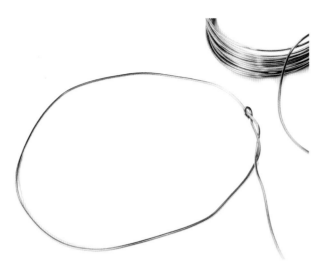

1. Using 12-gauge wire, create a loop slightly larger than the final crown size you want. With your fingers, loop the end wire around the oval shape to tie it together. Make sure to bend the wire's end into itself so it does not scratch or poke your head while the crown is being worn. Use your pliers to make the end loop around the loop to act as a knot. Note: Do not cut this wire until directed to do so.

2. Now that you have secured the first loop, create the top loop of the crown about 2" (5cm) above the first loop at the back and slightly higher in the front. This will add the height needed. Bring the wire all the way around to the back of the crown again and fold the wire onto itself so that the two loops will stay in order.

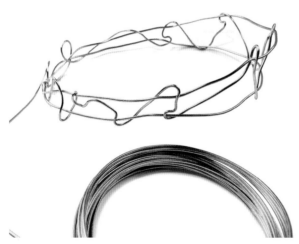

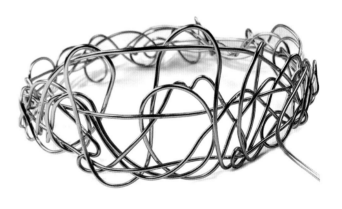

3. Pass the spool of wire in and out of the crown shape, attaching the wire loosely with bends and loops along the top and bottom loops. Bend the wire to start firming it into place. During this first pass around the crown, watch the shape to make sure you aren't pulling the wire too hard and flattening the height. Make little bends in the wire with your fingers or pliers to stiffen the structure. Don't cut the wire yet.

4. Repeat multiple times, around and around, in and out, filling in the space. Allow the wire to extend above and below the top and the bottom of the main form. Be generous with the wire, and tighten it up with bends as you go.

5. Once you are certain you are happy with how much wire you've used, bring the wire around to the back and cut it from the spool. Tuck the end into the crown so it will not come out, scratch, or poke. Loop it around another wire with pliers. Shape the entire piece with your hands to flatten, smooth, and create the final oval crown shape.

6. Using your pliers, make little one-quarter turns in the wire in various spots to firm it up. Go all the way around the crown. Then try the crown on. Does it still fit? Reshape the crown to fit your head, stretching it out if needed. Do any places poke you? Take the time to neaten the crown's fit before proceeding to the beading stage.

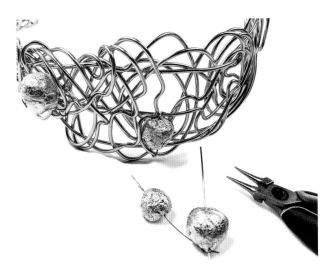

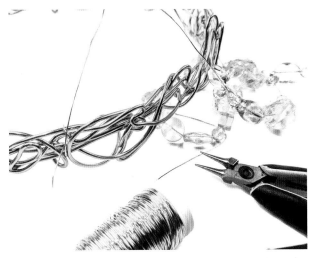

7. Start by placing individual bead links in a scattered pattern at the front of the crown, using 2" (5cm) pieces of 24-gauge wire. Use pliers to secure the bead links into place and flush cutters to trim off excess wire. Make sure no added wire will scratch your head.

8. String the rest of the beads that you want to incorporate onto the 24-gauge wire. This crown will be lightly beaded, with the beads mostly on the front portion. Tie the uncut 24-gauge wire onto the crown with a simple knot. Again, do not cut the wire from the spool until directed to do so. Trim the wire's tail and tuck it into itself to secure it and make sure that it will not scratch you.

9. Pass the beaded wire in and out of the crown, placing the beads where desired. Make sure no beads fall on the inside of the crown as you go; that would make it uncomfortable to wear. Pull slightly to keep most of the slack out of the wire as you go. You can backtrack and feed the wire in at different angles. Work the beads into your desired arrangement.

11. Using pliers, go through and gently push really visible wires back into the crown to make them less noticeable. Rearrange individual wires as desired. Slide your hands around it to shape it, flattening the sides and checking one last time for poking wires. Now enjoy being royalty with your new crown!

10. Once you are totally happy with the beads' locations, you can cut the wire from the spool. Firm up the wire with one-quarter turns with the pliers again. Don't pull so hard that you distort the crown; it is firm enough if the beads aren't moving around or sliding. When everything is firm, wrap the wire around a somewhat hidden part of the crown to secure the end, and trim it.

Bead Nests Necklace

I have been making these beaded wire circles, or bead nests, since I first started making jewelry. They are very much like hand sewing. You can make them in any shape or size, use any color of wire, and sew anything on them with a 24-gauge wire. You can make them into brooches, set them into rings, create earrings, necklaces, and bracelets, or even use them in headpieces. The featured necklace uses the sparkliest beads available: AB2X beads. It is glorious in person and nearly blinds you in the sun!

Skill level: Intermediate

Time: 5 hours

Safety notes: None

SUPPLIES

◊ Small AB2X bicone crystals (4mm)

◊ Scarab beads

◊ 12-gauge gold wire

◊ 24-gauge gold wire

◊ Jewelry pliers

◊ Flush cutters

◊ Head pin

◊ Lobster clasp

1. Collect a variety of colored beads to incorporate in your bead nests. Mix them all together in a single container to make the process easier and truly more random. Then cut an 8" (20cm) length of 12-gauge wire for each bead nest you want to create. I made 50 (you can see some of the bare wire circles I've made already in this photo).

2. Bend the wire into a small loop to get the base started. Holding the loop flat in one hand, use your other hand to continue looping the wire around the initial loop, keeping the shape flat. I am wearing gloves to keep the oil on my hands from transferring to the beads later, but this is optional.

3. Keep going until you've used the entire wire. It takes about four complete curls. Don't make the circles too tight or you will not be able to link them at the end. Keep the edges loose, but make sure there is wire in the very center so the beads have something to rest on later. Using pliers, tuck the wire ends into the base so they don't scratch. Repeat to make all the wire bases.

4. Since the beads I am using are small, I will need about 40 beads per bead nest, including at least one scarab bead per bead nest. Thread the beads onto the 24-gauge wire. Don't cut the wire off the spool yet.

5. Tie the end of the wire onto the wire base. Trim the end and tuck it into the base so it will not scratch.

6. Curl the beaded wire on top of the wire base so it creates a sort of bead nest. Now cut the wire from the spool, allowing at least 10" (25cm) of extra wire so you can sew the beads onto the wire base.

7. Gently sew the beads into place using the remaining wire, going up and down and around the entire wire base. Make sure all of the wired beads are secured. Pull the slack taut as you go.

8. This is the backside of the bead nest after sewing.

9. When all of the beads are secured, tie a knot to complete the sewing.

10. I kept the tail of the wire attached to each bead nest until the very end, as I wanted to use some of the tails to sew multiple bead nests together (such as for the earrings on page 145). Later, you can trim any extra wire off and tuck it into itself or into the nest of wires so it will not scratch. At this point, use pliers to add small one-quarter twists to the wire to firm it up.

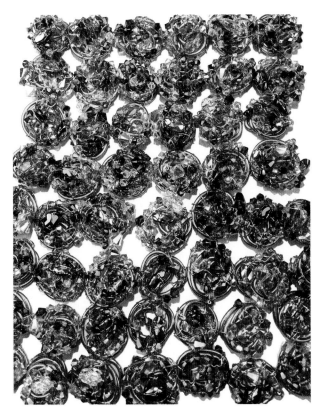

11. This photo shows the wires' tails trimmed. These bead nests are ready to be connected to the necklace!

12. Lay out the necklace and connect the bead nests with 4" (10cm) sections of 12-gauge wire looped like jump rings. Fold the jump rings so that they cannot come loose or poke. You could also use prepurchased jump rings instead. This photo shows the back of the connected necklace.

13. For the remainder of the necklace, use a few empty wire circles instead of a chain and attach a lobster clasp using a jump ring. Add a few beads to a head pin to create a flourish at the very end.

14. See how I have extra beads left over and did not use all 50 bead nests for the necklace? This necklace used 42 circles. The extra beads can be used for something else, and the other bead nests can be used for other projects (see below).

VARIATIONS

Partially fill a ring base with heavy-duty craft glue and nestle in a single finished bead nest.

Use different beads on your wire circles for a totally different look.

VARIATIONS

Create a simple drop necklace using one bead nest, jump rings, and a crystal AB drop. Thread the jump ring onto a chain.

Sew together three bead nests with the uncut tail wire, or use jump rings. One curl of 12-gauge wire at the top adds the earring hook.

Bead Nests Headpiece

Using several of the bead nests made for the Bead Nests Necklace on page 139, you can create a matching, stunning headpiece to make sure you're the center of attention.

Skill level: Intermediate

Time: 1 hour

Safety notes: None

SUPPLIES

◊ About 7 bead nests (see page 139)

◊ 12-gauge gold wire

◊ 24-gauge gold wire

◊ Jewelry pliers

◊ Flush cutters

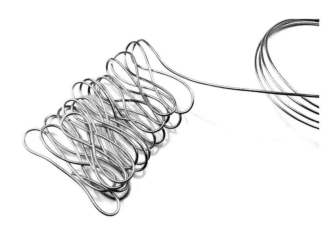

1. Start with an uncut spool of 12-gauge wire. Bend one end into a long loop with a pinched center as shown.

2. Continue bending the same kind of loop over and over, then push the loops together, overlapping them, until the entire piece is about 7" (18cm) long. Cut the wire from the spool.

3. Cut a piece of 24-gauge wire at least 20" (51cm) long. Tie one end of the wire to one end of the piece, tucking in the tip so that it doesn't scratch. Repeat with a second wire if desired.

4. Lay the bead nests onto the front of the piece and start sewing them on with the 24-gauge wire.

5. Double-check that each bead nest is secured to the piece. Tie off the remaining 24-gauge wire securely to the piece. Using your pliers, tighten the wire with small one-quarter turns on the front and the backside.

6. Create a side arm for the headpiece by cutting a 25" (64cm) length of 12-gauge wire and folding over about 6" (15cm) of it back onto itself, twisting it together to give it strength. Fold the end so it is secure and will not scratch. The remaining length will be used to attach the arm to the headpiece. Create a second matching arm.

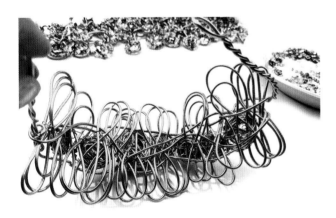

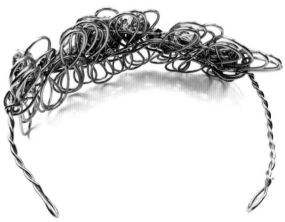

7. Thread one 12-gauge arm end through the headpiece all the way to the other side of the headpiece, going in and out of the loops. Repeat on the other side with the other arm. Tuck the ends in securely using your pliers.

8. Using your hands, smooth down the loops and form the piece into a headband shape. Double-check to make sure there are no wires that might scratch. You now have a headpiece with amazing sparkle!

Embellished Shark Teeth

I have been obsessed with fossils and teeth forever. My dad was a dentist, so that might explain part of my interest. Using epoxy clay and floral foam, you can easily embellish both sides of these stunning shark teeth at once. I didn't have enough black shark teeth, so I used nail polish to blacken one. Can you tell which one?

 Skill level: Easy

 Time: 1 hour plus curing time

 Safety notes: Work in a well-ventilated area; wear gloves

SUPPLIES

◊ Fossilized shark teeth (or replicas)

◊ Black epoxy clay

◊ Disposable gloves

◊ Baby wipes

◊ Plastic work surface

◊ Variety of clear crystal embellishments/rhinestones with foil backs

◊ Texturizing tool (any object desired)

◊ Black jump rings

◊ Floral foam

◊ For necklace: jewelry pliers, flush cutters, large jump rings, black chain, lobster clasp

1. Lay out an arrangement of shark teeth so you can see how your project will look when complete. Wearing gloves, mix the epoxy clay according to the manufacturer's instructions. Once mixed, make small logs out of the clay and use them to cover the top portion of each shark tooth on the front and the back.

2. Embed crystals into the clay on one side only.

3. Use the point of a pencil, a fork, or any other small item to add additional texture on the front and the back. The backs of these shark teeth, as you can see in later steps, are totally texturized. The tool I used is visible in the photo for step 2.

5. Place each tooth tip down into the floral foam and let the clay cure for 24 hours (or according to the manufacturer's instructions).

4. Embed a jump ring at least halfway into the clay on either side of the back of each tooth. When the clay cures, these will make the teeth super easy to link together. When you have finished embellishing, wipe the stones and the tooth with a baby wipe, being careful not to touch the clay with the wipe.

6. You can see here how each tooth back is totally texturized.

7. You can attach these ready-to-rock teeth to any jewelry piece. To make the featured necklace, simply link the teeth together with jump rings, add a small section of chain for the back of the necklace, and connect with a lobster clasp.

VARIATIONS

Use any extra black epoxy clay to quickly create a ring with a leftover gem. Make a ball with the clay, insert it into a ring base, and slowly push the stone into the clay.

I had enough stones left over to make a bracelet while I was at it. I used the same texturizing tool to match the texture of the bracelet.

This shark tooth not only has gems embedded in the clay at the top, but it was also decorated by dipping it in nail polish floating in a small tub of water. It's surprisingly easy to do—try it!

If all you have is smaller shark teeth, you can still make some toothy designs. This super-easy bracelet can be made following the basic technique shown on page 66.

154

Colorized Crystals

Clear quartz crystals are lovely, but I really wanted big pieces of aquamarine, which are expensive. So I bought a box of chunky clear quartz and used colored resin to create the look that I wanted. Experiment with colors to create your own rainbow of colored crystals!

⚙️ **Skill level:** Advanced

🕐 **Time:** 15 minutes per crystal plus curing and assembly time

🛡️ **Safety notes:** Work in a well-ventilated area; wear gloves

SUPPLIES

- ◊ Casting resin
- ◊ Resin dyes (I used yellow and blue)
- ◊ Wooden stir stick
- ◊ Marker
- ◊ Disposable measuring cup
- ◊ Disposable gloves
- ◊ Quartz crystals
- ◊ Floral foam

- ◊ 18-gauge brass wire
- ◊ Jewelry pliers
- ◊ Flush cutters
- ◊ Epoxy clay
- ◊ Beads/crystals
- ◊ Gold leaf
- ◊ Baby wipes

1. Gather all the resin supplies you will need: casting resin, resin dyes, a wooden stir stick, a marker, and a disposable measuring cup. Wearing gloves, mark the measuring cup for the two equal amounts you need to make the resin (following the manufacturer's instructions). Mix the resin according to the manufacturer's instructions.

2. It's time to add the dyes. Only add a few drops; if you dilute the mixture too much, it may not cure correctly. I used a drop of yellow and a few drops of royal blue to make an aqua shade. Stir well with the stick.

3. Check your color by testing it on the point of a crystal. Be warned: you only have a few minutes before the resin will start to cure, so work swiftly. The warmer the work area is, the faster the resin will cure.

4. Dip each crystal into the resin one time to coat it with tint. Don't worry too much about covering the entire crystal, unless you plan for the entire crystal to be visible in whatever project you have in mind.

5. After dipping, place each crystal into the floral foam with the point sticking up. The extra resin will drip down into the floral foam. At this point, use up any leftover resin if you can (in molds you have on hand, etc.). Allow the resin to fully cure for 24 hours or according to the manufacturer's instructions.

6. Once the crystals have cured, knock off any stuck floral foam with your fingers or a craft knife, but don't fuss over it too much, as the tops will be covered with clay later. Cut one 8" (20cm) piece of 20-gauge wire for each crystal.

7. Make a couple of loops around the top of each crystal with a wire. Don't pull it tight yet; you will tighten it at the end.

8. Create a loop over the top and tuck the ends under the other wire strands to secure it. Using pliers, gently twist the wire to remove slack, which will tighten it.

10. Wearing gloves, mix epoxy clay according to the manufacturer's instructions. Sculpt and coil a small snake around the top of each crystal. Also cover the wire loop with clay (see the photo in the next step).

9. Repeat to add a wire to every crystal.

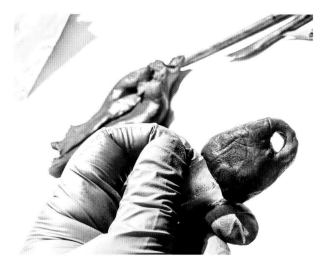

11. Make sure that the clay-covered wire loop at the top has a large enough hole that a jump ring can pass through it. Smooth all the clay with your fingers.

12. Press stones or beads into the clay as embellishments.

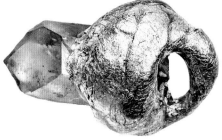

13. Cover all of the clay with a piece of gold leaf, smoothing it into the clay. Using a baby wipe, gently wipe away any gold foil on the beads and crystal.

14. Allow the clay to cure according to the manufacturer's instructions. Then use a brush to dust off any excess gold crumbs. See the color difference in the final piece? The top piece here has been colorized with resin, whereas the bottom has not.

VARIATIONS

One super-easy way to use these colorized crystals is to suspend a large one from a hoop and slide it onto a necklace. An instant stunner!

You don't have to embed embellishments into the clay; you can just cover it with gold leaf for a slightly tamer version.

You can use the same method described here on glass balls—just secure the wire to the ball with heavy-duty craft glue (such as E6000). You can put loops on the side and/or the top.

Feather Tassels

Feathers can be frustrating to try to incorporate into jewelry, as they don't exactly lend themselves to being attached to things. Use thermoplastic sheet to collect feathers together and make them easy to use in your jewelry.

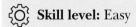 **Skill level:** Easy

Time: 5 minutes per tassel

Safety notes: Use caution when applying heat

SUPPLIES

◊ Black feathers

◊ Black 20-gauge wire

◊ Flush cutters

◊ Black thermoplastic sheet

◊ Scissors

◊ Craft heat gun/ embossing tool

◊ Silicone pad for work surface

◊ For necklace: black chain, variety of black and yellow beads, jump rings, clasp, embellished shark tooth

1. Cut a small rectangular piece of thermoplastic sheet that is about 1" x 2" (2.5 x 5cm). Cut a piece of wire about 3" (7.5cm) to 4" (10cm) long.

2. Gather the feathers into a bundle, lining up the ends. Wrap one end of the wire around the feathers two or three times to hold them together. Make sure no sharp wire ends are poking out that could scratch you. The remaining wire should be long enough to work with as a connector. You can always trim it later, but if it's too short, you're stuck.

3. Lay the small piece of thermoplastic sheet on top of the feather bundle and wire. Make sure the placement is nice and even.

4. Point the heat gun straight down at the thermoplastic sheet and turn it on. Watch carefully as the sheet slumps and slightly melts, then turn the heat off immediately.

5. You want the sheet to go soft, like a limp noodle. If you heat it up too much, it will shrink and bubble. Just let it gently begin to melt, then stop and wait for it to cool slightly so that you can touch it. This will only take a few seconds.

6. Using your fingers, gently roll the sheet completely around the feathers and wire. Pick up the bundle a bit so you can guide the foam under and around it. It should at least overlap. Roll the entire bundle against the silicone pad to smooth it out, but don't press too hard. The bundle will be warm to the touch but not hot. As it cools, it will start to stiffen. If it cools too quickly, just use a little more heat to soften it again.

7. The final product should look something like this—smooth and not too lumpy. These feather tassels are super lightweight. By bending the wire into a hook shape and giving it a little trim, you could wear these as instant earrings. I made half a dozen of these and used them on the featured necklace, which also includes an embellished shark tooth (see page 150).

BONUS IDEA

My craft knife needed to be upgraded or thrown out, but I loved it too much to just toss it. I covered it in thermoplastic sheet and then added a fresh blade. Perfect rehab!

165

FEATHER TASSELS

Wiggly Wire Cuff

I have been making these bracelets for many years. The thick wire is surprisingly easy to bend but holds its shape and color well. This project is dramatic, easy to wear, lightweight, and so fun to make. You don't even have to use beads!

⚙️ **Skill level:** Easy

🕐 **Time:** 30 minutes

🛡️ **Safety notes:** None

SUPPLIES

◊ 6-gauge gold wire

◊ Large-hole beads (to fit on the wire)

◊ Jewelry pliers

◊ Flush cutters

1. Slide about 12 beads onto the wire. These will be distributed over the cuff as you work.

2. Using your fingers or pliers, make a small loop to start to keep the beads from slipping off. Then make a bigger oval and keep one bead in this area.

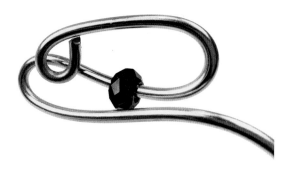

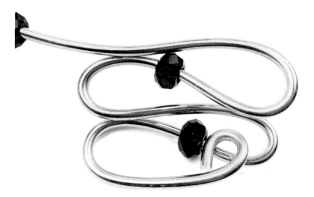

3. Now you will start looping in earnest, over and over. Make the loops about 3" (7.5cm) in height. Use your hands, go slowly, and watch your bracelet come alive. Start just by bending the wire back as shown.

4. Bend the wire back again and keep one bead in the loop. The beads in this design slide easily, which is part of the bracelet's charm.

168

5. Continue looping in this pattern, making sure that each loop is about the same size and has its own bead.

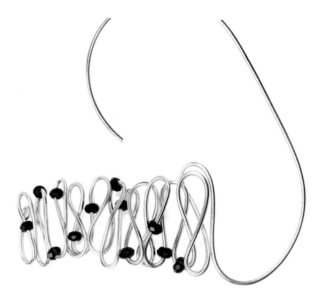

6. When you get to about 12 loops or have about 12" (30cm) of wire left, stop looping.

7. Heading in the opposite direction, weave the remaining wire under and over about every other loop, all the way back to the original first loop.

8. Flatten the loops slightly before you commit to finishing the bracelet. Check the bracelet to make sure all of the beads are spaced out nicely.

9. Using your pliers, curl the end of the wire onto the second or first loop you made.

10. Curve the bracelet into a cuff. Smooth it down with your hands and adjust the loops so that they look random but are still spaced out more or less equally. Now wear it with pride!

VARIATION

Use 12-gauge wire to make this bracelet by starting off with all the beads on the wire just like you did for the cuff. Start wrapping the wire around a form that is about the size of your wrist, distributing the beads as you go. When you're satisfied with the design, cut the wire off the spool, take the bracelet off the form, and wrap one of the wire ends around all the wraps to secure the shape of the bracelet. Secure both wire ends using pliers.

Ten-Minute Scarab Ring

This project is incredibly easy to whip up. Try making a whole collection of them as gifts, or one in every color to match any outfit!

Skill level: Easy

Time: 10 minutes plus curing time

Safety notes: Work in a well-ventilated area; wear gloves

SUPPLIES

◊ Ring base with high edge

◊ Flat-backed oval scarab bead or resin scarab casting

◊ Epoxy clay

◊ Disposable gloves

◊ Gold leaf

◊ Baby wipes

◊ Sealing spray or clear nail polish

1. Check the fit of your chosen scarab with the ring base. If it's too big and you can trim it, do so. If it's too small, you may want to choose another ring base or a different scarab. The final look is totally up to you, though. This resin scarab fit perfectly after a little trimming.

3. Roll the clay into a small log and fit it into the ring base.

2. Get the gold leaf out and ready. Wearing gloves, mix a small amount of epoxy clay according to the manufacturer's instructions.

4. Push the scarab into the ring and allow the extra clay to ooze out as you push down. Use your fingertips to smooth the edge up and over the scarab.

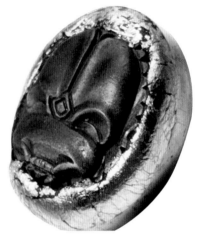

6. Clean off any clay that got onto the scarab with a baby wipe, being careful not to touch the clay or gold leaf with the wipe. Allow the clay to cure for 24 hours or according to the manufacturer's instructions. Seal with a sealing spray or clear nail polish.

5. Cover the clay with pieces of gold leaf. Smooth out the leaf until you are happy with the effect.

Index

Note: Page numbers in *italics* indicate projects.